AYRSH
STREET A

CONTENTS

Area of coverage & key to map symbols	2 - 3
Ardrossan, Saltcoats, Stevenston & index	4 - 9
Annbank, Mossblown & index	10 - 11
Ayr & Alloway	12 - 17
Auchinleck, Ballantrae, Barr,	18 - 19
Barrhill & indices	
Beith, Bellsbank & indices	20 - 21
Catrine, Colmonell, Coylton & indices	22 - 23
Crookedholm, Crosshill, Crosshouse,	24 - 25
Knockentiber & indices	
Cumnock, Dailly, Dalrymple & indices	26 - 29
Dalmellington, Drongan & indices	30 - 31
Dalry, Dunlop & indices	32 - 33
Darvel, Drybridge, Dundonald & indices	34 - 35
Fairlie, Fenwick, Hillhead & indices	36 - 37
Galston, Girvan & indices	38 - 39
Hurlford & index, Irvine	40 - 49
(includes Dreghorn & Springside)	
Kilbirnie (includes Glengarnock),	50 - 53
Kirkmichael, Kilmaurs & indices	
Kilmarnock & index	54 - 61

Kilwinning	62 - 63
Kirkoswald, Largs, Logan, Lugar & indices	64 - 67
Mauchline, Maidens & indices	68 - 69
Maybole, Minishant & indices	70 - 71
Millport & index	72 - 73
Muirkirk & index	74 - 75
New Cumnock & index	76 - 77
Newmilns, Ochiltree, Sorn & indices	78 - 79
Prestwick & Monkton	80 - 83
Patna, Skelmorlie & indices	84 - 85
Stewarton, Symington & indices	86 - 87
Tarbolton, Troon (includes Barassie)	88 - 91
& indices	
Turnberry	92
West Kilbride	93
Index section:	
Turnberry, West Kilbride	94
Ayr & Prestwick	94 - 99
(includes Alloway & Monkton)	
Irvine (includes Dreghorn & Springside)	99 - 101
Kilwinning	101 - 102

© Nicolson Digital Ltd 100057546
© Crown Copyright reserved.
The maps in this atlas are based upon the Ordnance Survey maps with the permission of Her Majesty's Stationery Office. All rights reserved. No part of this atlas may be reproduced, stored, or transmitted, in any form or by any means without the prior written permission of the publisher and copyright owners. The contents of this atlas are believed correct at the time of printing. However, no responsibility is accepted by the publishers for any errors or omissions, or changes in the detail given. The representation of a road, track or footpath is no evidence of a public right of way.
ISBN 978 0 99334 391 9

AREA OF COVERAGE & KEY TO MAP SYMBOLS

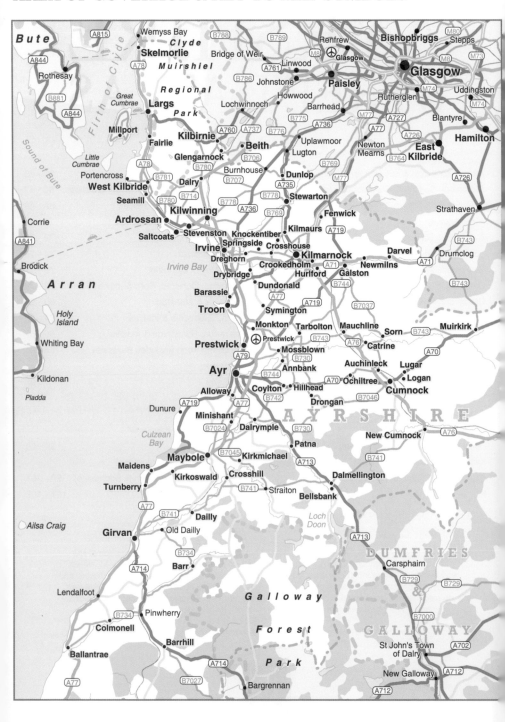

Symbol	Description	Symbol	Description
M77	Motorway	L	Library
A75	Primary route dual / single	PO	Post office
A79	A road dual / single	S	Superstore
B707	B road dual / single	B	Bus station
	Unclassified road	i	Tourist information centre
	Pedestrianised / one way street	a	Antiquity
	Long distance footpath	m	Museum
	Track / path		Castle
	Ferry route		Historic or visitable house
	Historic wall		Battlefield
	Railway / tunnel or disused rail		Garden
	Railway station		Caravan site
	Airport / heliport		Camping
▲	Primary school		Viewpoint
▼	Secondary school		Other tourist attraction
△	Special or independent school	✢	Church or place of worship
	Police station		Woodland
	Fire station		Park, recreation, sports or cemetery
	Ambulance station		Built up area
	Lifeboat station		Rocks
	Coastguard station		Shingle
H	Hospital		Sand
P	Parking		Marshland
F	Filling station		Mud

Scale 1:14000

0   500m

0   500yds

ARDROSSAN

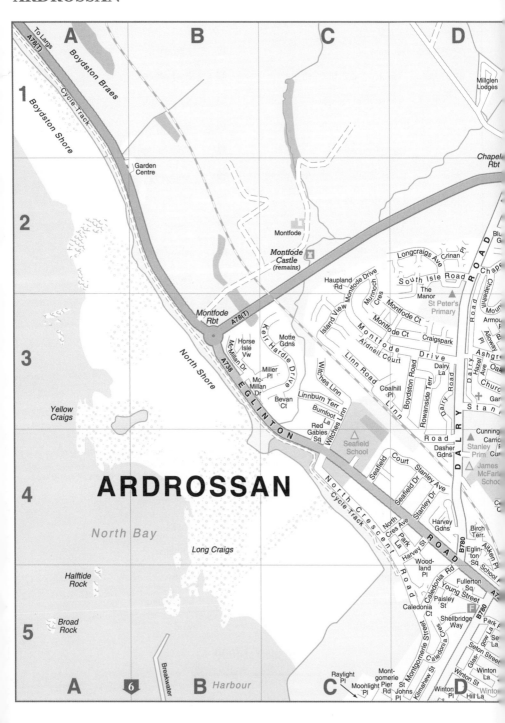

ARDROSSAN

North Bay

Long Craigs

North Shore

Yellow Craigs

Halftide Rock

Broad Rock

Boydston Braes

Boydston Shore

Cycle Track

To Largs
A78(T)

Garden Centre

Millglen Lodges

Chapel Rbt

Montfode

Montfode Castle (remains)

Montfode Rbt

A78(T)

A738

EGLINTON

Haupland Rd

Montfode Drive

Island View

Munnoch Cres

Longcraigs Ave

Crinan Pl

South Isle Road

The Manor

St Peter's Primary

Montfode Ct

Montfode Ct

Craigspark

Montfode Drive

Ardnell Court

Linn Road

Dalry La

Coalhill Pl

Linn

Boydston Road

Rowanside Terr

Dalry Road

Churc

Gar

Stan

Keir Hardie Drive

Horse Isle Vw

Motte Gdns

Miller Pl

Mc-Millan Dr

McMillan Dr

Bevan Ct

Witches Linn

Linnburn Terr

Burnfoot La

Witches Linn

Red Gables Sq

Seafield School

Seafield

Seafield Court

Seafield Dr

Stanley Dr

Stanley Ave

North Cres Ave

Park La

Harvey St

North Crescent Road

Cycle Track

Dasher Gdns

Road

Cunning

Carric

Stanley

Prim Cur

James McFarla Schoo

Harvey Gdns

Birch Terr.

Woodland Pl

Caledonia Rd

Young Street

Paisley St

Caledonia Ct

Fullerton Sq

Shellbridge Way

Montgomerie Street

Kilmahew St

Caledonia Cres

Winton St

Winton Pl

St Johns Pl

Montgomerie Pier Rd

Raylight Pl

Moonlight Pl

Broad Rock

Breakwater

DALRY ROAD

ROAD

B780

B780

Eglinton Sq

School

Aitken Pl

Winton La

Seton Street

Seton La

Hill La

Park

Ashgr

Hazel Ave

Oak

Armou

Alloway Pl

Chapelhill

Road

ROAD

Blu G

Chape

Mour

Harbour

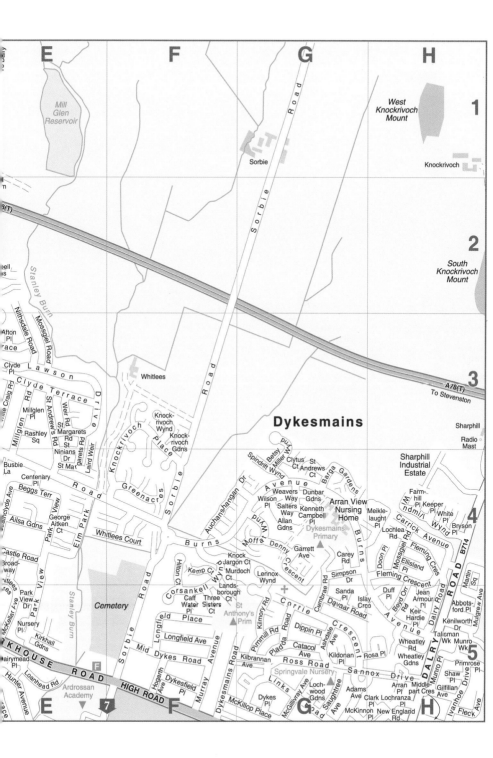

E   **F**   **G**   **H**

1

Mill Glen Reservoir

West Knockrivoch Mount

Knockrivoch

2

South Knockrivoch Mount

Sorbie

Stanley Burn

Nithsdale Road

Mossgiel Road

Afton Pl

Clyde Pl

Clyde Terrace

Lawson Drive

Whitlees

Knock-rivoch Wynd

Knock-rivoch Gdns

A78(T)
To Stevenston

3

Sharphill

Radio Mast

Dykesmains

Millglen Pl

St Andrew's Rd

Weir Rd

St Margarets Rd

St Rd

Laird Weir

Rashley Sq

Ninians Dr

St Mat

Garrets Rd

Millglen

ttie Craig Rd

Busbie La

Centenary Pl

Beggs Terr

nchyde Ave

Ailsa Gdns

George Aitken Ct

Park View

Elm Park

Knockrivoch Road

Greenacres

Sorbie

Sorbie Road

Whitlees Court

Burns

Auchanshangan Dr

Spindrift Wynd

Betsy Miller Ct

Clytus Ct

St Andrews Ct

Barga Gardens

Sharphill Industrial Estate

Farm-hill Pl

Keeper Pl

Windmill Wynd

White Pl

Bryson Pl

Carrick Avenue

Weavers Way

Dunbar Gdns

Salters Way

Kenneth Campbell Pl

Allan Gdns

Arran View Nursing Home

Meiklelaught Pl

Lochlea Rd

Avenue

Wilson Pl

Moffat Wynd

Dykesmains Primary

Doon Pl

Mossgiel Pl

Fleming Cres

Ellisland Pl

Garrett Ave

Carey Rd

Burns

Lochinazia

Fleming Crescent

Castle Road

Broad-way

itilees res

Park View Dir

Nursery Pl

Kirkhall Gdns

airymead Pl

Stanley Burn

Cemetery

Hilton Ct

Knock Jargon Ct

Kemp Ct

Murdoch Ct

Lennox Wynd

Simpson Dr

Cumbrae Rd

Sanda Pl

Islay Cres

Duff Pl

Jean Armour Pl

Keir Hardie Pl

Boyd Orr

Dalry Road

Martin Sq

Mulgrew Ave

Corsankell Wynd

Caff Pl

Three Sisters Ct

Lands-borough Ct

Davaar Road

Corrie

Avenue

Abbots-ford Pl

Kenilworth Dr

St Anthony's Prim

Kilnoy Rd

Dippin Pl

Corrie

Crescent

Ashdale Ave

Talisman Wk

Munro Wk

Wheatley Rd

eld Place

Longfield Ave

Longfield Ave

Mid Dykes Road

Sorbie Road

Hogarth Pl

Dykesfield Pl

Murray Avenue

Pirnmill Rd

Plada Pl

Catacol Ave

Kilbrannan Ave

Ross Road

Kildonan Pl

Rosa Pl

Wheatley Gdns

Primrose Pl

Shaw Pl

Gilfillan Ave

KHOUSE ROAD

HIGH ROAD

Ardrossan Academy

F

Links

Dykesmains Road

McKillop Place

Dykes Pl

McGillivray Ave

Springvale Nursery

Loch-wood Gdns

Saughtree Rd

Adams Ave

Sannox Drive

Clark Pl

Arran Middle-part Cres

Ivanhoe Drive

Munro Pl

Dalry Road

B714

Loanhead Rd

Hunter Avenue

McKinnon Pl

New England Rd

Fleck

E   **7**   **F**   **G**   **H**

ARDROSSAN & SALTCOATS

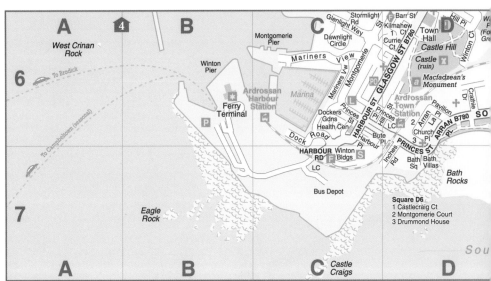

Index to Ardrossan

Abbotsford Place	H5
Adair Avenue	G6
Adams Avenue	G5, G6
Acids Road	Q10
Afton Court	L7
Afton Place	E3
Afton Road	L6
Ailsa Drive	K7
Ailsa Gardens	E4
Ailsa Road	H6
Aitken Place	D4
Alexander Avenue	M5
Alexander Place	L6
Allan Gardens	G4
Alloway Place	D3
Anderson Drive	H6
Anderson Terrace	D5
Ardchoille Drive	M5
Ardchoille Lane	M5
Ardeer Lane	N9
Ardlui Terrace	H7
Ardneil Court	C3
Ardoch Court	M9
Ardoch Crescent	M9
Ardoch Terrace	M8
Ardrossan Road	F7
Argyle Place	F7
Argyle Road	G7
Armour Place	D3
Arran Court	K7
Arran Lane	D6
Arran Place	D6, H5
Arthur Street	H8, L7
Arthurlie Place	F7
Ashdale Avenue	G5
Ashenyards Park	P5
Ashgrove Avenue	M5
Ashgrove Road	D3
Auchanshangan Drive	F4
Auchenharvie Place	J6

Auchenharvie Road	H7
Barga Gardens	G4
Barnett Court	G8
Barnett Crescent	G8
Barony Court	D6
Barr Street	D6
Barra Place	N5
Barrie Terrace	E5, E6
Bath Square	D7
Bath Villas	D7
Beattie Court	L8
Beggs Terrace	E4
Berchem Place	G7
Betsy Miller Wynd	G4
Bevan Court	C3
Birch Terrace	D4
Blakely Road	J8
Bluebell Gardens	D2, E2
Boglemart Street	K7
Bonnie Lesley Court	L7
Border Avenue	G7
Border Place	G7
Boyd Orr Road	H5
Boydston Road	D3
Bradshaw Street	G8
Braehead Lane	G7
Braehead Place	G7
Braes Road	F8
Bridgepark	E6
Broadway	E4
Brown Place	G6
Bryson Place	H4
Burma Road	P10
Burn Road	E7
Burnbank Street	L7
Burnfoot Lane	C3
Burnlea Place	M5
Burns Avenue	F4, G4, H5
Burns Place	M6
Burns Square	E3
Burns Terrace	D3
Burnside Place	L6

Busbie Lane	E4
Bute Court	K7
Bute Place	D6
Bute Terrace	F6
Byrehill Drive	P5
Caff Water Place	F5
Caledonia Court	D5
Caledonia Crescent	D5
Caledonia Road	D5, F6
Caledonian Road	M8
Caley Court	L8
Cambuskeith Road	M4
Campbell Avenue	F7, L5
Canal Court	H8
Canal Crescent	L8
Canal Place	H8
Canal Street	H8
Canal View	H8
Caponcraig Avenue	K6
Carey Road	G4
Carment Drive	M8
Carmyle Place	L8
Carrick Avenue	H4
Carrick Place	D4
Castle Avenue	M4
Castle Road	E4
Castlecraig Court (1)	D6
Castlehill Farm	P4
Castlehill Road	N5
Catacol Avenue	G5
Centenary Place	E4
Central Avenue	E4, P10
Central Quadrant	D4
Chapelwell Street	G8
Chaplehill Mount	D2
Christie Gardens	G7
Church Place	D6
Churchill Drive	D3
Clark Crescent	L8
Clark Place	H5
Clements Place	M5
Clyde Place	E3

Clyde Terrace	E4
Clyde View Avenue	
Clytus Court	K7
Coalhill Place	D6
Corrie Crescent	F6
Corsankell Wynd	P5
Countess Street	F5
Craigdene Drive	D5
Craigs Place	D5, F6
Craigspark	
Crathie Drive	L8
Crinan Place	M4
Cumbrae Road	
Cumbrae Terrace	H8
Cunninghame Crescent	L8
Cunninghame Drive	
Cunninghame Road	
Currie Court	D
Dairymead Place	
Dalry Lane	
Dalry Road	
(Ardrossan)	D
Dalry Road	
(Stevenston)	
Darg Road	
Dasher Gardens	
Davaar Road	
Dawnlight Circle	
Deer Park Avenue	
Denny Crescent	
Diddup Drive	
Dippin Place	
Dock Road	
Dockers Gardens	
Dockhead Place	
Dockhead Street	
Donaldson Avenue	G
Doon Place	
Drummond House (3)	
Dubbs Road	
Duff Place	
Duguid Drive	

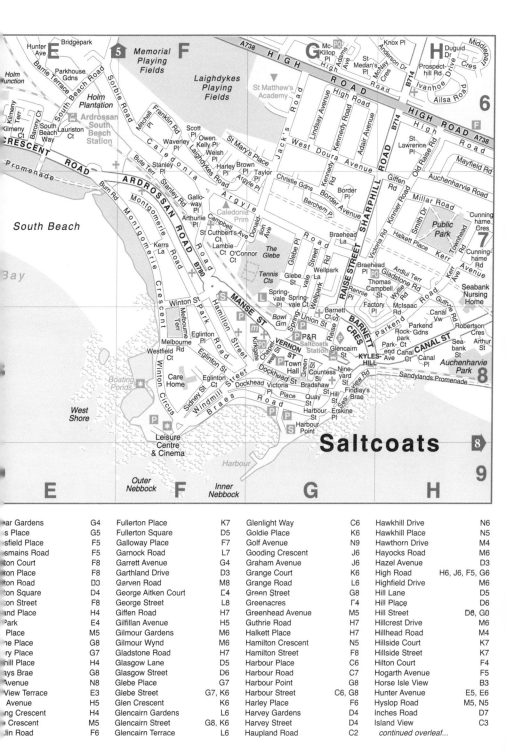

ar Gardens	G4	Fullerton Place	K7	Glenlight Way	C6	Hawkhill Drive	N6
s Place	G5	Fullerton Square	D5	Goldie Place	K6	Hawkhill Place	N5
sfield Place	F5	Galloway Place	F7	Golf Avenue	N9	Hawthorn Drive	M4
smains Road	F5	Garnock Road	L7	Gooding Crescent	J6	Hayocks Road	M6
ton Court	F8	Garrett Avenue	G4	Graham Avenue	J6	Hazel Avenue	D3
ton Place	F8	Garthland Drive	D3	Grange Court	K6	High Road	H6, J6, F5, G6
ton Road	D3	Garven Road	M8	Grange Road	L6	Highfield Drive	M6
ton Square	D4	George Aitken Court	C4	Green Street	G8	Hill Lane	D5
ton Street	F8	George Street	L8	Greenacres	F4	Hill Place	D6
and Place	H4	Giffen Road	H7	Greenhead Avenue	M5	Hill Street	D6, G0
Park	E4	Gilfillan Avenue	H5	Guthrie Road	H7	Hillcrest Drive	M6
Place	M5	Gilmour Gardens	M6	Halkett Place	H7	Hillhead Road	M4
ne Place	G8	Gilmour Wynd	M6	Hamilton Crescent	N5	Hillside Court	K7
ry Place	G7	Gladstone Road	H7	Hamilton Street	F8	Hillside Street	K7
hill Place	H4	Glasgow Lane	D5	Harbour Place	C6	Hilton Court	F4
ays Brae	G8	Glasgow Street	D6	Harbour Road	C7	Hogarth Avenue	F5
View Terrace	E3	Glebe Place	G7	Harbour Point	C6	Horse Isle View	B3
Avenue	H5	Glebe Street	G7, K6	Harbour Street	C6, G8	Hunter Avenue	E5, E6
ng Crescent	H4	Glen Crescent	K6	Harley Place	F6	Hyslop Road	M5, N5
Crescent	M5	Glencairn Gardens	L6	Harvey Gardens	D4	Inches Road	D7
lin Road	F6	Glencairn Street	G8, K6	Harvey Street	D4	Island View	C3
		Glencairn Terrace	L6	Haupland Road	C2	*continued overleaf...*	

STEVENSTON

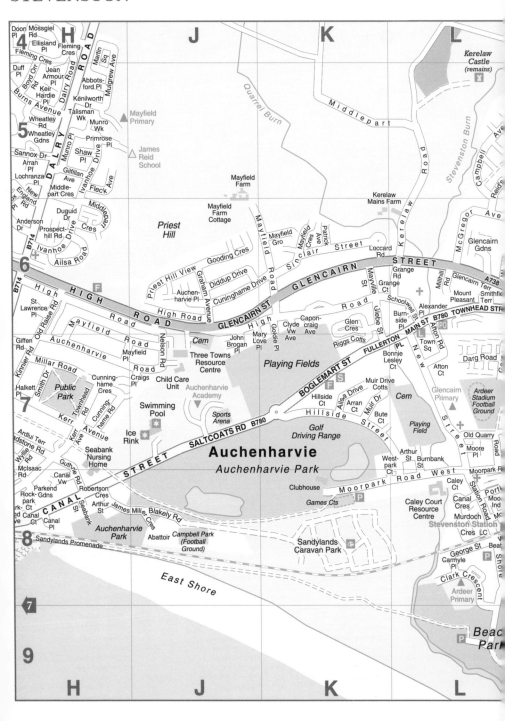

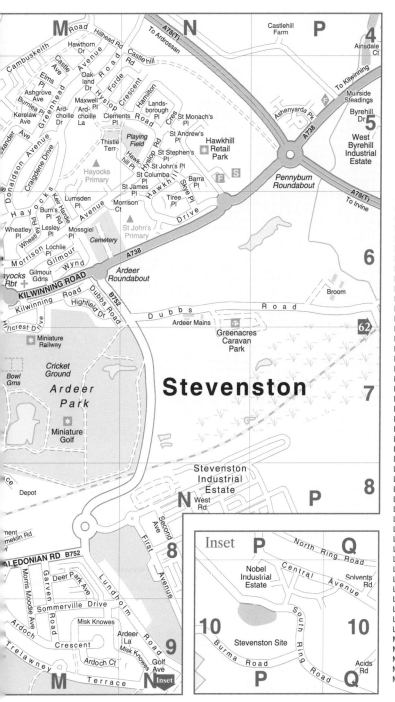

continued from overleaf...

Islay Crescent	G5
Ivanhoe Drive	H5
Jacks Road	G6
James Miller Crescent	H8
Jean Armour Place	H5
John Brogan Place	J7
Keeper Place	H4
Keir Hardie Drive	C3
Keir Hardie Place	H5
Keir Hardie Road	M6
Kemp Court	F4
Kenilworth Drive	H5
Kennedy Road	G6
Kenneth Campbell Place	G4
Kerelaw Avenue	M5
Kerelaw Road	L6
Kerr Avenue	H7
Kerrs Lane	F7
Kilbrannan Avenue	G5
Kildonan Place	G5
Kilmahew Court	D6
Kilmahew Street	D5
Kilmeny Court	E6
Kilmeny Terrace	E6
Kilmory Road	G5
Kilwinning Road	M6
Kinnier Road	H7
Kirkgate	G8
Kirkhall Gardens	E5
Knock Jargon Court	F4
Knockrivoch Gardens	F3
Knockrivoch Place	F3
Knockrivoch Wynd	F3
Knox Place	H6
Kyleshill	G8
Laighdykes Road	F6
Laird Weir	E4
Lambie Court	F7
Landsborough Court	F5
Landsborough Place	N5
Lauriston Court	E6
Lawson Drive	E3
Lennox Wynd	G4
Lesley Place	M6
Limekiln Road	M8
Lindsay Avenue	G6
Links Road	G5
Linn Road	C3
Linnburn Terrace	C3
Loanhead Road	E5
Loccard Road	K6
Lochlea Road	H4
Lochlie Place	M6
Lochranza Place	H5
Lochwood Gardens	G5
Longcraigs Avenue	D2
Longfield Avenue	F5
Longfield Place	F5
Lumsden Place	M6
Lundholm Road	M8
McDowall Avenue	E5
McDowall Place	E4
McGillivray Avenue	G5
McGregor Avenue	L6
McIsaac Road	H7

continued overleaf...

9

ANNBANK & MOSSBLOWN

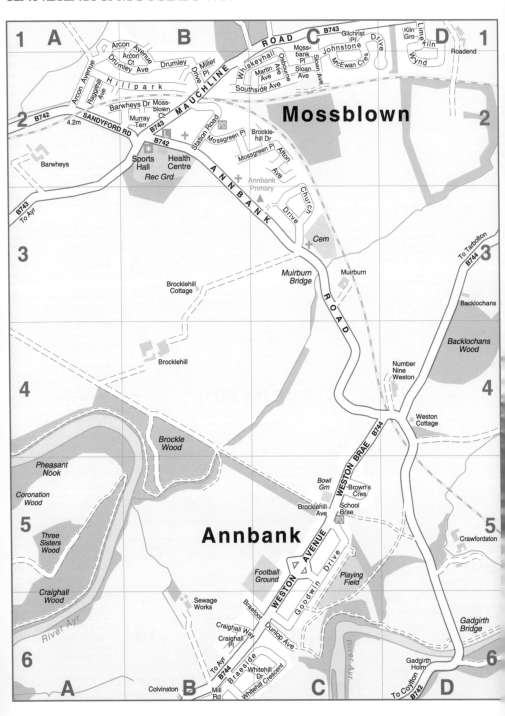

continued from overleaf...

cKellar Avenue	E5
cKillop Place	F5, G6
cKinnon Place	H5
cMillan Drive	B3
cNay Crescent	G6
ain Street	L6
anor, The	D2
anse Street	F7
ariners View	C6
artin Square	H4
ary Love Place	J6
axwell Place	M5
ayfield Crescent	K6
ayfield Grove	K6
ayfield Place	H7
ayfield Road	H6, K6
ayville Street	K6
eiklelaught Place	H4
elbourne Road	F8
elbourne Terrace	F8
d Dykes Road	F5
ddlepart Crescent	H6
ddlepart	K5
l Farm	E2
lar Road	H7
ler Place	C3
lglen Lodges	D1
lglen Place	E3
lglen Road	E3
lhill Road	L6
sk Knowes	M9
chell Place	F6
ffat Wynd	C4
ntfode Court	D3
ntfode Drive	C3
ntgomerie Court (2)	D6
ntgomerie Crescent	F7
ntgomerie Pier	C5
oad	
ntgomerie Road	F7
ntgomerie Street	C6, D5
onlight Place	C5
ore Place	L7
orpark Place	L8
orpark Road East	L7
orpark Road West	K8
ris Moodie Avenue	M8
rison Avenue	M6
rison Court	M6
ssgiel Place	
ssgiel Road	E3, H4
te Gardens	C3
nt Pleasant	L6
r Drive	K7
r Drive Cottages	K7
rside Steadings	P5
grew Avenue	H5
noch Crescent	C3
ro Place	H5
ro Walk	H5
doch Court	F4
doch Crescent	L8
ray Avenue	F5
son Road	J7
England Road	H5
Street	L7
yard Street	G8

Nithsdale Road	E3
North Crescent Avenue	D4
North Crescent Road	C4
North Ring Road	P9
Nursery Place	E5
Oak Road	D3
Oakland Drive	M5
O'Connor Court	F7
Old Quarry Road	L7
Old Raise Road	H6
Owen Kelly Place	F6
Paisley Street	D5
Park Lane	D4
Park Road	D5, F8
Park View	E5
Park View Drive	E5
Parkend Avenue	H8
Parkend Gardens	H8
Parkend Road	H8
Parkhouse Gardens	E6
Parkhouse Road	E5
Patrick Avenue	K6
Pavilion Place	D6
Pirnmill Road	G5
Pladda Road	G5
Portland Place	L8
Priest Hill View	J6
Primrose Place	H5
Princes Place	C6
Princes Street	C6, D6
Prospecthill Road	H6
Quay Street	G8
Queen's Drive	E4
Raise Street	G6, G7
Rashley Square	E3
Raylight Place	C5
Red Gables Square	C4
Reid's Avenue	L5
Rennie Place	G7
Riggs Cottages	K7
Roberston Crescent	H8
Rockpark Court	H8
Rosa Place	H5
Ross Road	G5
Rowanside Terrace	D3
St Andrews Court	G4
St Andrew's Place	N5
St Andrew's Road	E3
St Columba Place	N5
St Cuthbert's Court	F7
St James Place	N5
St John's Place	D5, N5
St Laurence Place	H6
St Margaret's Road	E3, E4
St Mary's Place	F6
St Meddan's Place	G6
St Monach's Place	N5
St Ninian's Drive	E3
St Stephen's Place	N5
Saltcoats Road	J7
Salters Way	G4
Sanda Place	G5
Sandylands Promenade	H8
Sannox Drive	G5
Saughtree Avenue	G5
School Place	D5
Schoolwell Street	L6
Scott Place	F6

Seabank Street	H8
Seafield Court	C4
Seafield Drive	D4
Seaview Road	G8
Second Avenue	N8
Seton Lane	D5
Seton Street	D5
Sharphill Road	G7
Shaw Place	H5
Shellbridge Way	D5
Shore Road	L8
Simpson Drive	G4
Sinclair Street	K6
Skye Place	N5
Smith Drive	H7
Smithfield Terrace	L6
Solvents Road	Q10
Sommerville Drive	M9
Sorbie Road	E6, F4, F5, G2
South Beach	E6
Road	
South Beach Way	E6
South Crescent	D6
Road	
South Isle Road	D2
South Ring Road	P10
Spindrift Wynd	G4
Springvale Court	G7
Springvale Place	G7
Springvale Street	G8
Stanley Avenue	D4
Stanley Drive	D4
Stanley Place	F6
Stanley Road	D3, F7
Station Road	L8
Stormlight Road	C6
Strathclyde Avenue	E4
Sydney Street	F8
Talisman Walk	H5
Taylor Place	G7
Thistle Terrace	M5
Thomas Campbell	H7
Street	
Three Sisters Court	F5
Tiree Place	N6
Town Square	L7
Townhead Road	H7
Townhead Street	L6
Trelawney Terrace	M9
Union Street	G8
Vernon Street	G8
Verona Place	E6
Victoria Place	G8
Victoria Road	G7
Wallace Avenue	L6
Warner Street	L8
Waverley Place (1)	F6
Weavers Way	G4
Weir Road	E3
Wellpark Lane	G7
Wellpark Road	G7
Welsh Place	F6
West Doura Avenue	G6
West Park Court	K7
West Road	N8
Westfield Court	F8
Wheatley Gardens	H5
Wheatley Place	M6

Wheatley Road	H5, M6
White Craig Road	E3
White Place	H4
Whitlees Court	F4
Whitlees Crescent	E4
Wilson Place	G4
Windmill Street	F8
Windmill Wynd	H4
Winton Buildings	C7
Winton Circus	F8
Winton Court	D6
Winton Lane	D5
Winton Place	D5
Winton Street	D5, F7
Witches Linn	C3
Woodland Place	D4
Wyllie Road	H7
Young Street	D5

Index to Mossblown & Annbank

Afton Avenue	C2
Annbank Road	B2
Arcon Avenue	B1
Arcon Court	B2
Barwheys Drive	A2
Braefoot	B6
Braeside	B6
Brocklehill Avenue	C5
Brocklehill Drive	C2
Brown's Crescent	C5
Church Drive	C3
Craighall Place	B6
Craighall Way	B6
Drumley Avenue	A2
Drumley Drive	B2
Dunlop Avenue	C6
Gadgirth Holm	D6
Gilchrist Place	C1
Goodwin Drive	C6
Hillpark	A2
Johnstone Drive	C1
Kiln Grove	D1
Limekiln Wynd	D1
McEwan Crescent	C2
Martin Avenue	C2
Mauchline Road	B2
Mill Road	B6
Miller Place	B2
Mossbank Place	C2
Mossblown Court	B2
Mossgreen Place	B2
Murray Terrace	B2
Osbourne Avenue	C2
Raggethill Avenue	A2
Sandyford Road	A2
School Brae	C5
Sloan Avenue	C2
Southside Avenue	B2
Station Road	B2
Weston Avenue	C6
Weston Brae	C5
Whiskeyhall	B2
Whitehill Crescent	B6
Whitehill Drive	C6

AYR

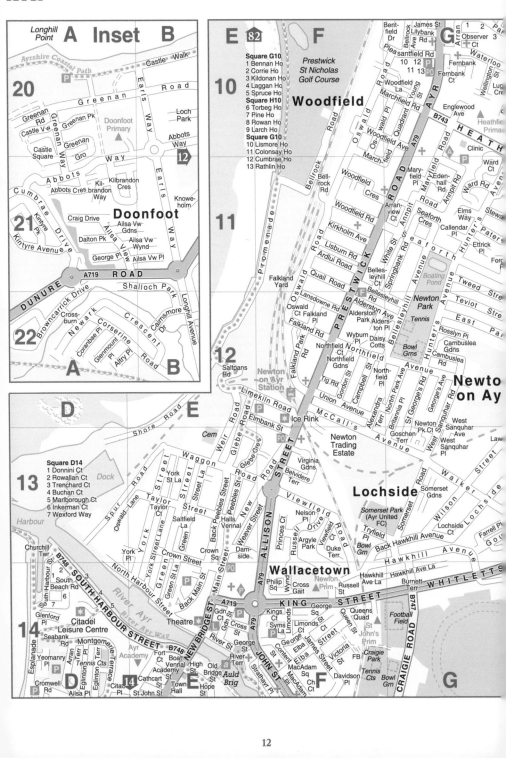

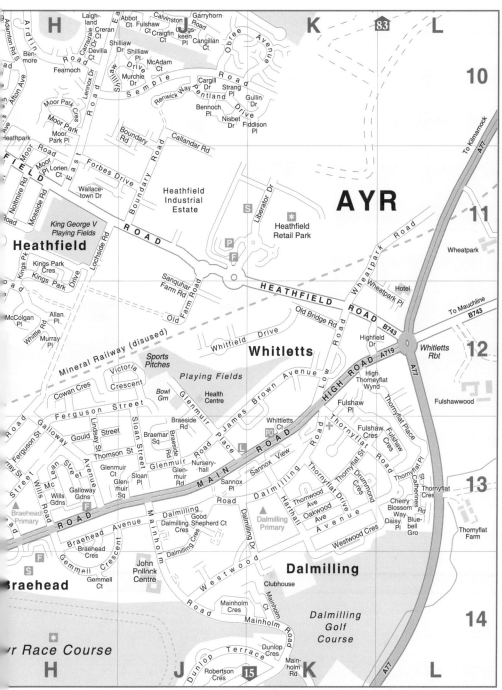

Index to street names can be found starting on page 94

AYR

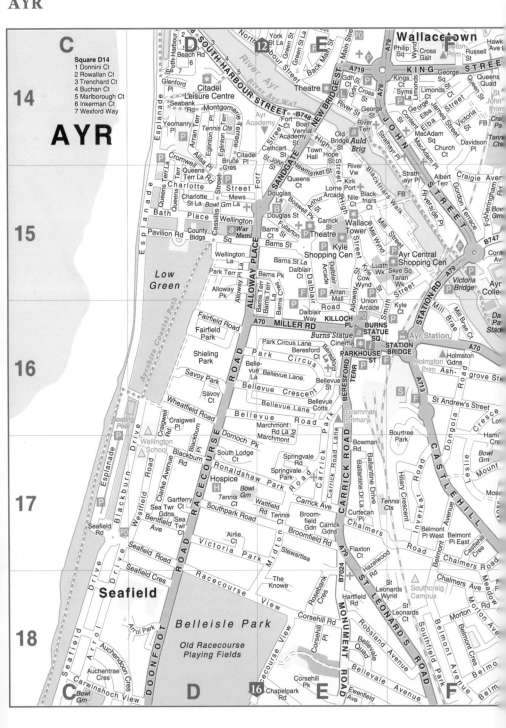

Square D14
1 Donnini Ct
2 Rowallan Ct
3 Trenchard Ct
4 Buchan Ct
5 Marlborough Ct
6 Inkerman Ct
7 Wexford Way

14

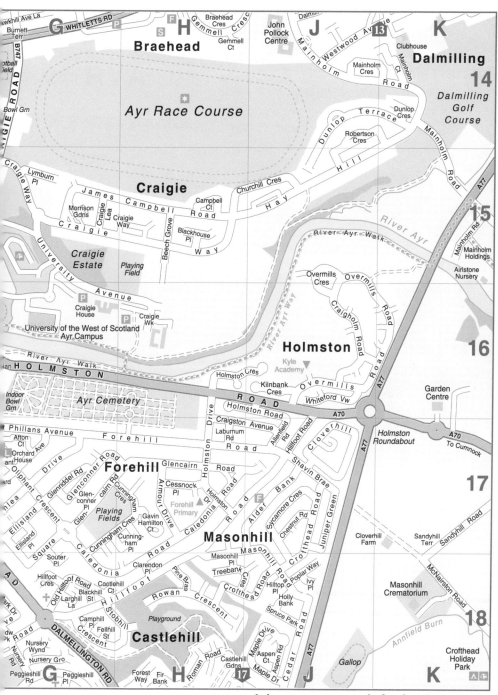

Ayr Race Course

Braehead

Dalmilling

Dalmilling Golf Course

Craigie

Craigie Estate

University of the West of Scotland Ayr Campus

River Ayr

Holmston

Ayr Cemetery

Forehill

Masonhill

Castlehill

Holmston Roundabout

To Cumnock

Masonhill Crematorium

Crofthead Holiday Park

Gallop

Annfield Burn

14
15
16
17
18

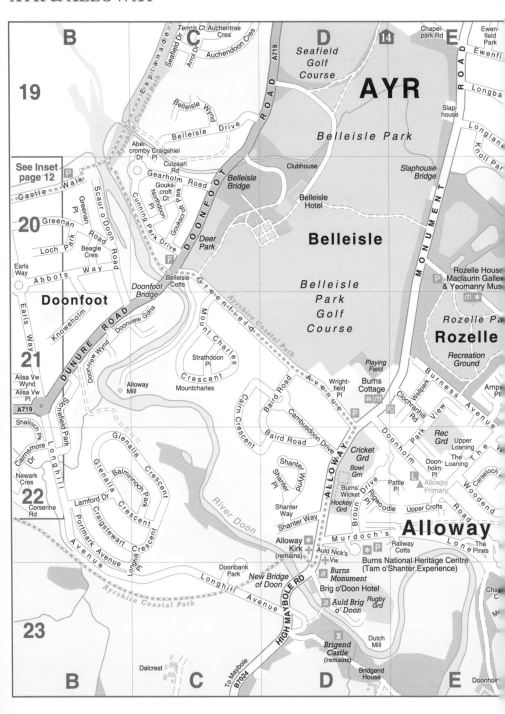

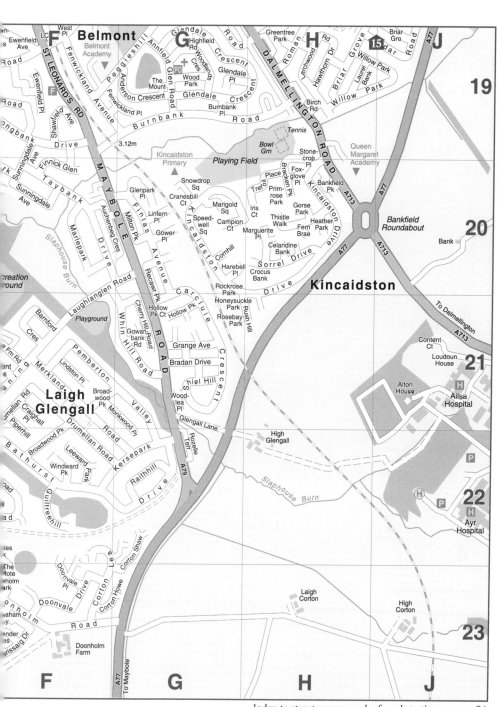

Index to street names can be found starting on page 94

17

AUCHINLECK, BALLANTRAE, BARR & BARRHILL

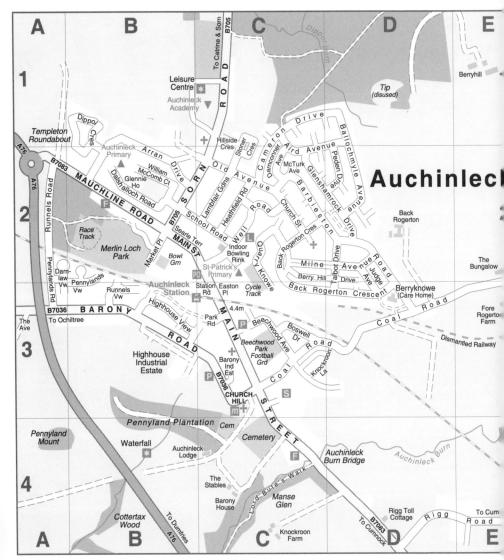

Index to Auchinleck

Aird Avenue	C2	Church Hill	C3	Judge Avenue	D2
Arran Drive	B1	Church Street	C2	Knockroon Lane	C3
Avenue, The	A3	Coal Road	C3, D3	Lambfair Gardens	C2
Back Rogerton Crescent	C2	Dalshalloch Road	B2	Lord Bute's Walk	C4
Ballochmyle Avenue	D1	Darnconner Avenue	C2	McTurk Avenue	C2
Barbieston Road	C2	Darnlaw View	A2	Main Street	B2, C3
Barony Road	B3	Dippol Crescent	B1	Market Place	B2
Beechwood Avenue	C3	Easton Place	C3	Mauchline Road	B2
Berry Hill Drive	C2	Glennie House	B2	Milne Avenue	C2
Boswell Drive	C3	Glenshamrock Drive	C2	Old Avenue	C2
Cameron Drive	C2	Heathfield Road	C2	Park Road	C3
		Highhouse View	B3	Peden Drive	D2
		Hillside Crescent	C1	Pennylands Road	A2

Pennylands View	D2
Quarry Knowe	C2
Rigg Road	C4
Runnels Road	A2
Runnels View	C2
School Road	C2
Searle Terrace	B2
Sorn Road	B2
Station Road	C3
Stoner Crescent	C2
Talbot Drive	C2
Well Road	C2
William McComb Court	A2

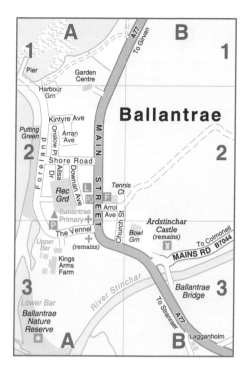

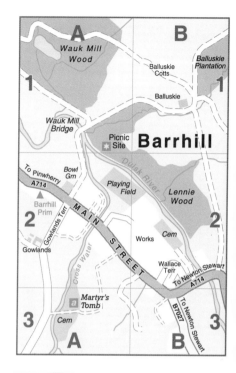

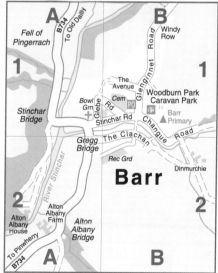

Index to Ballantrae

Ailsa Drive	A2
Arran Avenue	A2
Arrol Avenue	A2
Church Street	A3
Downan Avenue	A2
Foreland	A2
Harbour Green	A2
Kintyre Avenue	A2
Main Street	A2
Mains Road	B3
Onslow Place	A2
Shore Road	A2
Vennel, The	A3

Index to Barr

Avenue, The	B1
Changue Road	B1
Clachan, The	B1
Glebe Road	A1
Glenginnet Road	B1
Stincher Road	A1
Windy Row	B1

Index to Barrhill

Balluskie Cottages	B1
Gowlands Terrace	A2
Main Street	A2
Wallace Terrace	B2

BEITH & BELLSBANK

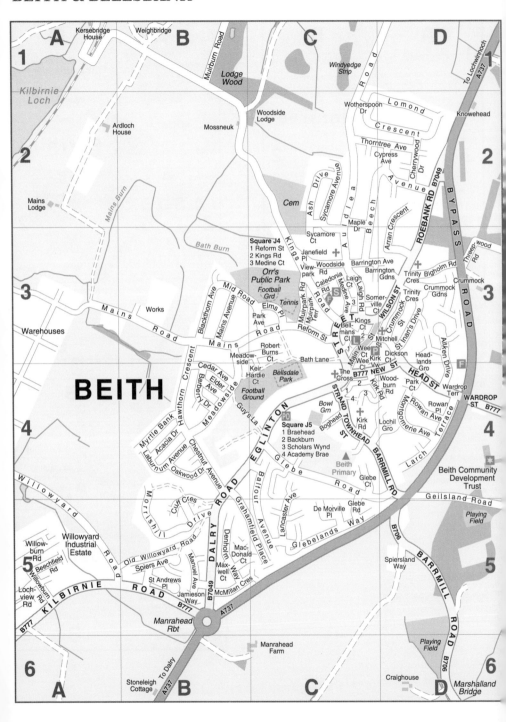

BEITH

Square J4
1 Reform St
2 Kings Rd
3 Medine Ct

Square J5
1 Braehead
2 Backburn
3 Scholars Wynd
4 Academy Brae

Kilbirnie Loch

Kersebridge House

Weighbridge

Muirburn Road

Lodge Wood

Windyedge Strip

To Lochwinnoch

A737

Ardloch House

Mossneuk

Woodside Lodge

Wotherspoon Dr

Lomond

Crescent

Knowehead

Thorntree Ave

Cypress Ave

Cherrywood Dr

Mains Lodge

Mains Burn

Cem

Ash

Drive

Sycamore Avenue

Auldlea

Beech

Avenue

Arran Crescent

ROEBANK RD

B7049

BYPASS

Bath Burn

Kings

Orr's Public Park

Football Grd

Tennis

Sycamore

Maple Dr

Janefield Pl

View-park

Woodside Rd

Caledonia Ct

Barrington Ave

Barrington Gdns

Laigh Ct

Laigh Rd

Medine Ave

Trinity Cres

Bigholm Rd

Threep-wood Rd

Crummock Rd

Crummock Gdns

Crummock

Trinity Cres

Somer-ville Ct

Mid Road

Elms Pl

Park Ave

Works

Mains Avenue

Blackthorn Ave

Muirpark Rd

Muirpark Terr

Reform St

Road

R S

Mains Road

Road

Reform St

Kings Ct

Bell-mans Cl

Mitchell St

St Inan's Drive

Aitken Drive

F

Warehouses

Robert Burns Ct

Meadow-side

Bath Lane

Wee Ct

Wee Ct Vw

Dickson Ct

Kirk Ct

Head-lands Gro

Cedar Ave

Elder Ave

Barberry Dr

Keir Hardie Ct

Bellsdale Park

Football Ground

The Cross

B777

NEW ST

Wood-burn Rd

Park Ct

HEAD ST

Wardrop Terr

Rowan Pl

Montgomerie Ave Terrace

WARDROP ST

B777

Myrtle Bank

Hawthorn Crescent

Meadowside

Guy's La

STRAND

TOWNHEAD ST

Bowl Grn

Boghead

Square J5

Kirk Rd

Lochil Gro

Rowan Ave

Larch

Acacia Dr

Laburnum Avenue

Chestnut Avenue

Oakwood Dr

EGLINTON ROAD

Glebe

Beith Primary

Glebe Rd

Glebe Ct

Beith Community Development Trust

Geilsland Road

Playing Field

Morrishill

Cuff Cres

Drive

DALRY ROAD

Balfour Avenue

Grahamfield Place

Lancaster Ave

De Morville Pl

Glebe Rd

Glebelands Way

BARRMILL RD

B706

Willowyard

Willow-burn Rd

Willowyard Industrial Estate

Beechfield Rd

Willowburn Rd

Old Willowyard Road

Spiers Ave

St Andrews Pl

Manuel Rd

Denholm

Mac-Donald Ct

Max-well Ct

Way

McMillan Cres

B7049

Spiersland Way

BARRMILL

ROAD

B706

Playing Field

Loch-view Rd

KILBIRNIE

ROAD

B777

Jamieson Way

A737

Manrahead Rbt

Stoneleigh Cottage

To Dalry

A737

Manrahead Farm

Craighouse

Marshalland Bridge

dex to Beith

acia Drive	B4
ademy Brae (4)	C4
ken Drive	D3
an Crescent	D3
n Drive	C2
ldlea Road	C3
ckburn (2)	C4
four Avenue	C4
rberry Drive	B4
rrington	C3
venue	
rrington	D3
ardens	
rmill Road	C4, D5
h Lane	C3
ech Avenue	C3
echfield Road	A5
lmans Close	C3
holm Road	D3
ckthorn	B3
enue	
ghead	C4
ehead (1)	C4
ass Road	D2
edonia Road	C3
lar Avenue	B4
rrywood Drive	D2
estnut Avenue	B4
ss, The	C4
mmock	D3
ardens	
mmock Street	D3
f Crescent	B5
ress Avenue	D2
ry Road	B5
Morville Place	C5
holm Way	B5
kson Court	D3
nton Street	C4
er Avenue	B4
s Place	C3
sland Road	D4
ne Court	C4
ne Road	C4, C5
elands Way	C5
namfield	B5
ace	
's Lane	B4
thorn	B4
escent	
d Street	D4
dlands Grove	D3
eson Way	B5
efield Place	C3
Hardie Court	C4
rnie Road	A5
s Court	C3
s Road (2)	C3

Kirk Road	C4
Kirk View	C3
Laburnum Avenue	B4
Laigh Court	C3
Laigh Road	C3
Lancaster Avenue	C5
Larch Terrace	D4
Lochil Grove	D4
Lochview Road	A5
Lomond Crescent	D2
MacDonald Court	B5
McMillan	B5
Crescent	
Main Street	C3
Mains Avenue	B3
Mains Road	A3, B3
Manuel Avenue	B5
Maple Drive	C2
Maxwell Court	B5
Meadowside	B3, B4
Medine Avenue	C3
Medine Court (3)	C3
Mid Road	B3
Mitchell Street	D3
Montgomerie	D4
Avenue	
Morrishill Drive	B5
Muirburn Road	B1
Muirpark Road	C3
Muirpark Terrace	C3
Myrtle Bank	B4
New Street	C4
Oakwood Drive	B4
Old Willowyard	B5
Road	
Park Avenue	C3
Park Court	D4
Reform Street (1)	C3
Robert Burns	C3
Court	
Roebank Road	D3
Rowan Avenue	D4
Rowan Place	D4
St Andrews Place	B5
St Inan's Drive	D3
Scholars Wynd (3)	C4
Somerville Court	C3
Spiers Avenue	B5
Spiersland Way	D5
Strand	C4
Sycamore Avenue	C2
Sycamore Court	C3
Thorntree Avenue	C2
Threepwood Road	D3
Townhead Street	C4
Trinity Crescent	D3
Viewpark	C3
Wardrop Street	D4
Wardrop Terrace	D4
Wee Close	C3

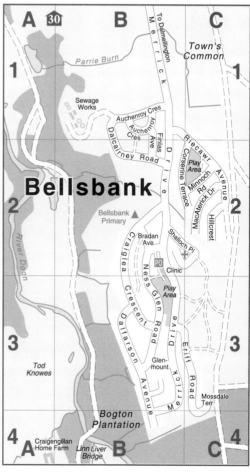

Wee Court	C3
Willowburn Road	A5
Willowyard Road	A4
Wilson Street	D3
Woodburn Road	D4
Woodside Road	C3
Wotherspoon Drive	C2

Index to Bellsbank

Auchenroy Crescent	B1
Bradan Avenue	B2
Corserine Terrace	C2
Craiglea Crescent	B2
Dalcairney Road	B1
Dalfarson Avenue	B3

Eriff Road	C3
Finlas Avenue	B1
Glenmount	B3
Hillcrest	C2
MacAterick Drive	C2
Merrick Drive	B1, B3
Minnoch Road	C2
Mossdale Terrace	C3
Ness Glen Road	B2
Riecawr Avenue	C1
Shalloch Place	B2

CATRINE, COLMONELL & COYLTON

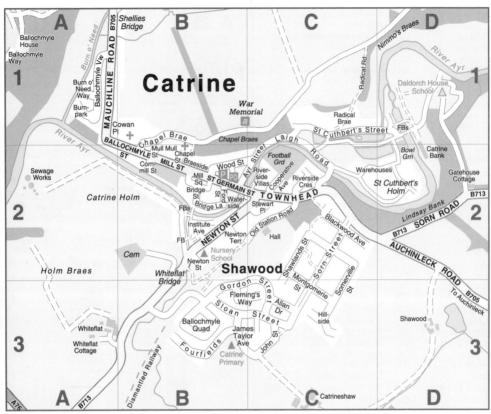

Index to Catrine

Allan Drive	C3	Institute Avenue	B2
Auchinleck Road	D2	James Taylor Avenue	B3
Ayr Street	B2	John Street	C3
Ballochmyle House	A1	Laigh Road	C1
Ballochmyle Quadrant	B3	Mauchline Road	A1
Ballochmyle Street	B2	Mill Square	B2
Ballochmyle View	A1	Mill Street	B2
Ballochmyle Way	A1	Montgomerie Street	C3
Blackwood Avenue	C2	Mull Mull Street	B2
Braeside	B2	Newton Street	B2
Bridge Lane	B2	Newton Terrace	B2
Bridge Street	B2	Old Station Road	C2
Burn o' Need Way	A1	Radical Brae	C1
Burnpark	A1	Radical Road	C1
Chapel Brae	B1	Riverside Crescent	C2
Chapel Street	B2	Riverside Villas	C2
Cooperative Avenue	C2	St Cuthbert's Street	C1
Cornmill Street	B2	St Germain Street	B2
Cowan Place	A1	Shawlands Street	C2
Fleming's Way	B3	Sloan Street	B3
Ford Street	B2	Somerville Street	C3
Fourfields	B3	Sorn Road	D2
Gordon Street	B3	Sorn Street	C2
Hillside	C3	Stewart Place	C2
		Townhead	C2
		Waterside	B2

Wood Street	B2		

Index to Coylton

Arthurston Terrace	A2	Gallowhill Quadrant	B1
Ashgrove	B2	Garvine Road	B2
Ayr Road	A2	Glenhead Court	C2
Barclaugh Drive	A2	Glenhead Place	C3
Barngore Drive	B2	Hamilton Place	B3
Beeches, The	B2	Highpark Road	B3
Broadwood	B2	Hillhead	D2
Bryden Place	C3	Hole Road	B2
Burgoyne Drive	B2	John Hodge Court	B2
Carnell Drive	B2	Kyle Crescent	B1
Carrick View	B1	Laighpark Court	A2
Chestnut Grove	B2	Laighpark Road	A2
Coats Place	B3	Laighpark View	A2
Dalblair Crescent	B2	Lochfergus Crescent	B3
Dalrymple View	B3	Lochfergus Drive	B3
Douglas Brown Place	B3	Lochfergus Place	B3
Douglas Road	B2	Lochfergus Wynd	B3
Drumcoyle Drive	B1	Martnaham Drive	B2
Drumsuy Court	B3	Meadow Park	B2
Fergus Way	B2	Milton Park	B2
Gadgirth Court	B2	Murray Park	B2
Gallowhill Farm	B2	Park Terrace	B2
		Parklands	B2
		Potterhill Place	B3
		Ramseyston Avenue	B2
		St Brides Way	C3

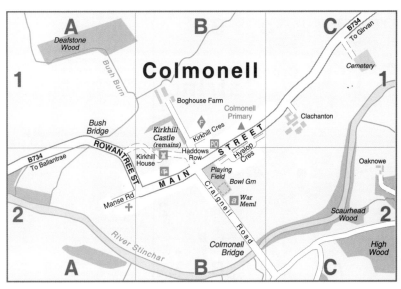

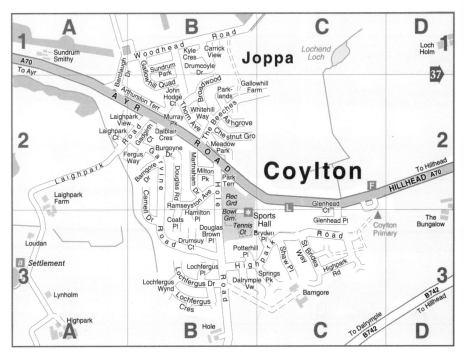

CROOKEDHOLM, CROSSHILL, CROSSHOUSE & KNOCKENTIBEI

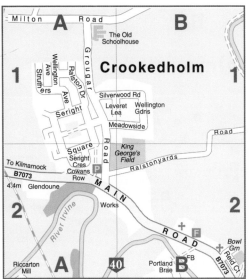

Reid Court	B2
Seright Crescent	A1
Seright Square	A1
Silverwood Road	A1
Struthers Avenue	A1
Wellington Avenue	A1
Wellington Gardens	B1

Index to Crosshouse & Knockentiber

Annandale Court	C4
Annandale Crescent	C3, C4
Annandale Gardens	B4
Annandale House	C4
Annandale Lane	B4
Annandale View	C4
Barr Avenue	C1
Busbie Cottages	B3
Busbie Gardens	B5
Busbie View	B4
Carmel Place	A4
Castle Terrace	C2
Corse Place	C5
Craig Drive	B5
Craigie Place	C5
Craiglea Avenue	B4
Craufurdhill Place	A4

Credon Drive
Crossdene Road
Crosshouse Road
Dean Place
Fisher Court
Fisher Way
Fardalehill View
Gatehead Road
Greenhill Terrace
Hannah Drive
Hemphill View
Hunter Road
Irvine Road
Kilmarnock Road
Kilmaurs Road
Laigh Milton Road
Laurieland Avenue
Loudoun Place
Mote View
Parkhill Avenue
Plann Cottages
Plann Road
Playingfield Crescent
Playingfield Road
South Windyedge
Southhook Road
Springfield Road
Springhill Avenue
Thornton Avenue
Woodbank Road
Woodlea Court
Woodlea Crescent
Wyndford Cottages

Index to Crookedholm

Cowans Row	A2
Glendoune	A2
Grougar Road	A1
Leveret Lea	A1
Main Road	A2
Meadowside	A1
Milton Road	A1
Portland Brae	B2
Ralston Drive	A1
Ralstonyards Road	B2

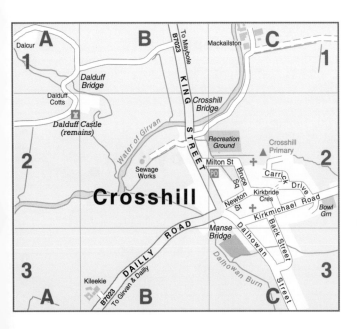

Index to Crosshill

Back Street	C2
Bruce Square	C2
Carrick Drive	C2
Dailly Road	B3
Dalduff Cottages	A2
Dalhowan Street	C2
King Street	B1
Kirkbride Crescent	C2
Kirkmichael Road	C2
Milton Street	C2
Newton Street	C2

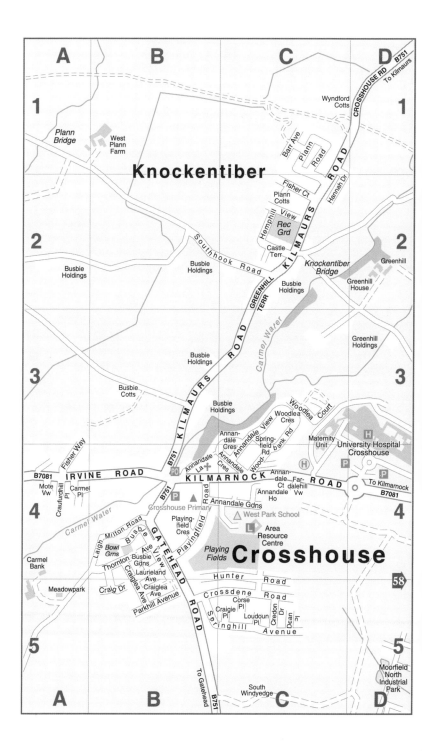

A   **B**   **C**   **D**   B751

1

Wyndford Cotts

CROSSHOUSE RD   To Kilmaurs

1

Plann Bridge

West Plann Farm

Barr Ave

Plann Road

R O A D

Knockentiber

Fisher Ct

Plann Cotts

Hannah Dr

View

Hemphill View

Rec Grd

K I L M A U R S

2

Busbie Holdings

Busbie Holdings

Southhook Road

Castle Terr

Knockentiber Bridge

Greenhill

2

Busbie Holdings

Greenhill House

GREENHILL TERR

R O A D

Carmel Water

Greenhill Holdings

3

Busbie Cotts

Busbie Holdings

Busbie Holdings

K I L M A U R S

Woodlea View

Woodlea Cres

Woodlea Court

Greenhill Holdings

3

Fisher Way

Annan-dale Cres

Annandale View

Spring-field Rd

Bank Rd

Maternity Unit

H

University Hospital Crosshouse

P

B7081   **I R V I N E   R O A D**

Annandale La

Annandale Cres

Wood

Annan-dale Ct

Far-dalehill

H

R O A D

P

To Kilmarnock B7081

Mote Vw

Craufurdhill Pl

Carmel Pl

K I L M A R N O C K

Annandale Vw

Annandale Ho

4

Carmel Water

Annandale Gdns

Crosshouse Primary

P

West Park School

4

Laigh

Milton Road

Busbie

Busbie Ave

Playing-field Cres

Playingfield Rd

L

Area Resource Centre

Carmel Bank

Bowl Grns

Thornton

Busbie Gdns

Craiglea Ave

G A T E H E A D

Playing Fields

Crosshouse

Meadowpark

Craig Dr

Laurieland Ave

Craiglea Ave

Parkhill Avenue

Hunter Road

Crossdene Road

Corse

58

R O A D

Craigie Pl

Springhill

Loudoun Pl

Credon Dr

Dean Dr

Avenue

5

Moorfield North Industrial Park

5

To Gatehead

South Windyedge

B751

A   **B**   **C**   **D**

CUMNOCK

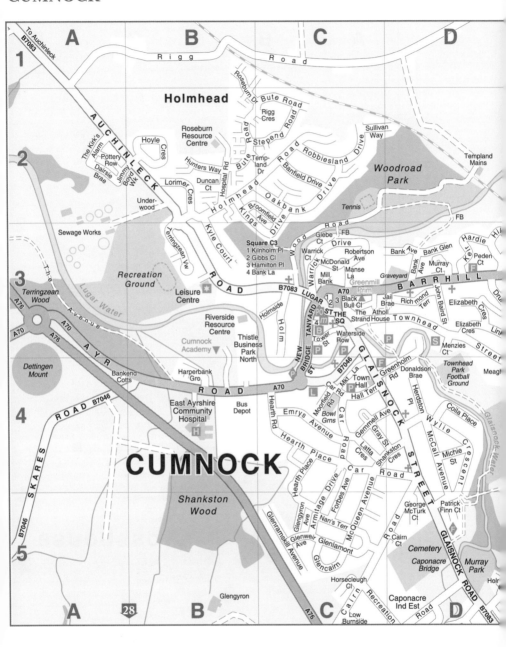

Index to Cumnock

Armitage Drive	C5	Glenlamont	C5	
Atholl Hosue	C3	Glenmuir Road	F3	
Auchinleck Road	A2	Glenramskill Avenue	C5	
Avenue, The	A3	Glenweir Avenue	C5	
Avisyard Avenue	F6	Gray Street	C4	
Ayr Road	A3	Greenholm Road	D4	
Ballantyne Court	E3	Hall Terrace	C4	
Banfield Drive	C2	Hamilton Place (3)	C3	
Bank Avenue	D3	Harperbank Grove	B4	
Bank Glen	D3	Hearth Place	C4	
Bank Lane (4)	C3	Hearth Road	C4	
Bankend Cottages	A4	Hemmings Way	F4	
Barrhill Road	D3	Herdston Place	D4	
Barrhill Terrace	E3	Hillside View	E4	
Barshare Road	E4	Hillview Court	F4	
Birchwood Road	E4	Holland Crescent	E3	
Black Bull Close	C3	Holm	C3	
Blackfaulds Road	E6	Holmburn Avenue	E5	
Broomfield Avenue	B2	Holmburn Close	D5	
Buntens Road	E7	Holmburn Place	E6	
Bute Road	B2, C2	Holmburn Road	E5, E6	
Cairn Court	D5	Holmhead Road	B2	
Cairn Road	A7, C5	Holmside	C3	
Cairnscadden Road	F6	Horsecleugh Close	C5	
Cameron Crescent	D6	Hospital Road	B2	
Campbell Court	E4	Hoyle Crescent	B2	
Caponacre Road	D6	Hunter's Way	B2	
Car Road	C4	Jail Brae	D3	
Carsgailloch Avenue	E6	James Young Avenue	E6	
Church Court	E6	Jimmy Boyd Walk	A2	
Coila Place	D4	John Allan Drive	D6	
Craigens Place	E6	John Baird Street	D3	
Craigens Road	E6	John Weir Avenue	E4	
Dairsie Brae	A2	Jubllee Court	E4	
Dalgleish Avenue	E3	Keir Hardie Hill	D3	
Davaar Avenue	F6	Kilbrennan Avenue	F7	
Donaldson Brae	D4	Kings Drive	B2	
Drumbrochan Road	D3	Kings Way	E4	
Dumfries Road	E7	Kilnholm Place (1)	C3	
Duncan Court	B2	Kirk's Alarm, The	A2	
Edgar Avenue	E4	Kyle Court	B3	
Elizabeth Crescent	D3	Lamont Crescent	E6	
Emrys Avenue	C4	Latta Crescent	C4	
Forbes Avenue	C5	Link Road	D3	
Gemmell Avenue	C4	Lorimer Crescent	B2	
George McTurk Court	D5	Low Burnside	C5	
Gibbs Close (2)	C3	Lugar Street	C3	
Glaisnock Glen	E7	McCall Avenue	D4	
Glaisnock Road	D5, E7	McClymont Court	E3	
Glaisnock Street	C3	McDonald Street	C3	
Glaisnock View	E6	McIntyre Crescent	F6	
Glebe Court	C3	McQueen Avenue	C5	
Glencairn	C5	McTurk Road	E6	
Glengyron Avenue	C5	Manse Lane	C3	
		Market Lane	C4	
		Meagher Court	D4	

continued overleaf...

CUMNOCK, DAILLY & DALRYMPLE

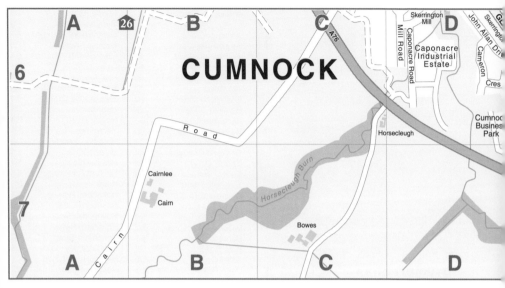

Index to Dailly

Back Road	B2, C1
Bridge Street	B2
Brunston Avenue	A1
Brunston Wynd	A2
Church Crescent	C2
Eldinton Terrace	B2
Golf Course Road	A2
Greenhead Street	C1
Hadyard Terrace	C2
Hazelwood Avenue	C2
Linfern Road	C1
Loaning, The	C2
Main Street	B2, C2
Smith Crescent	B2
Victory Crescent	C1
West End	B2
Wood Street	B2
Woodside	B2

Index to Dalrymple

Barbieston Court	B2
Barbieston Courtyard	C3
Barbieston Road	B2
Barbieston Terrace	C3
Birch Avenue	B3
Burnside Drive	B2
Burnton Court	B2
Burnton Road	B2
Cedar Terrace	B3
Church Street	
Doonvale Avenue	
Forglen Road	
Fulton Place	
Garden Street	
Glebe Avenue	
Glebe Cottages	
Hillview	
Holms Farm Road	
Kirkton Avenue	
McTaggart View	

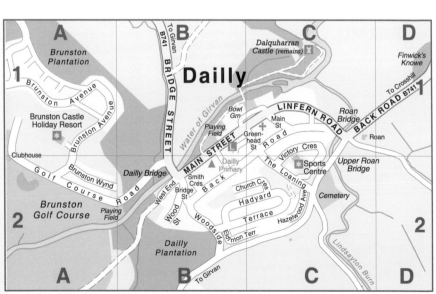

Index to Cumnock

continued from overleaf...

Menzies Avenue	E6
Menzies Court	D3
Michie Street	D4
Mill Bank	C3
Mill Road	D6
Moorfield Road	C4
Muirkirk Road	F3
Murray Court	D3
Nans Terrace	C5
Netherthird Place	E6
Netherthird Road	E6
New Bridge Street	C4
Oakbank Drive	C2
Patrick Finn Court	D5
Phillips Wynd	E7
Peden Court	D3
Penders Wynd	E7
Pottery Row	A2
Recreation Road	C5
Richmond Terrace	D3
Rigg Crescent	C2
Rigg Road	B1
River View	E4
Robbiesland Drive	C2
Robertson Avenue	C3
Roseburn Drive	B1
Ryderston Drive	E6
Shankston Crescent	C4
Skares Road	A4
Skerrington	E7
Skerrington Place	D6
Square, The	C3
Stepend Road	C2
Strand, The	C3
Sullivan Way	C2
Tanyard	C3
Templand Drive	C2
Terringzean View	B3
Tower Street	C3
Townhead Street	D3
Tweedlie Court	E6
Underwood	B2
Walker Court	E3
Warrick Court	C3
Warrick Drive	C3
Waterside Row	C3
Wood Road	C3
Wylie Crescent	D4

Index to Dalrymple continued...

Main Street	A3
Maxwell Place	C2
Merkland Drive	C2
Millbank Street	B2
Morton Drive	C2
Portland Road	B3
Primpton Avenue	B2
Purclewan Crescent	B2
Riverside Terrace	A3
Robertson Place	C2
Seath Drive	B2
Skeldon Crescent	B3
Skeldon Drive	B3
Viaduct View	C3
Weir Terrace	B2

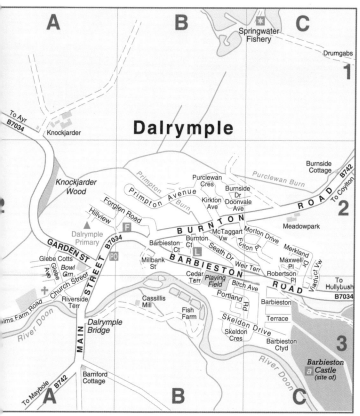

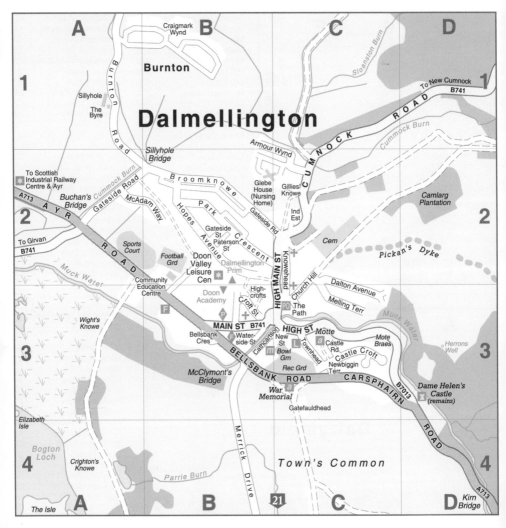

Index to Dalmellington

Armour Wynd	B1	Craigmark Wynd	B1	McAdam Way	A2
Ayr Road	A2	Croft Street	B3	Main Street	B3
Bellsbank Crescent	B3	Cumnock Road	C2	Melling Terrace	C3
Bellsbank Road	B3	Dalton Avenue	C2	Merrick Drive	B4
Broomknowe	B2	Gatefauldhead	C3	New Street	C3
Burnton Road	A1	Gateside Road	A2, B2	Newbiggin Terrace	C3
Carsphairn Road	C3	Gateside Street	B2	Park Crescent	B2
Castle Croft	C3	Gillies' Knowe	C2	Paterson Street	B2
Castle Road	C3	High Main Street	C3	Path, The	C3
Cathcartson	B3	High Street	C3	Townhead	C3
Church Hill	C3	Highcrofts	B3	Waterside Street	B3
		Hopes Avenue	B2		
		Knowehead	C2		

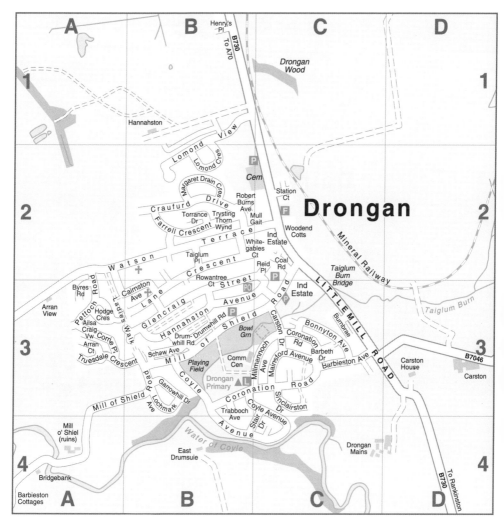

Index to Drongan

Ailsa Craig View	A3	Corrie Place	A3	Lomond Crescent	B2	Rowantree Court	B2
Arran Court	A3	Coyle Avenue	B3	Lomond View	B2	Schaw Avenue	B3
Barbeth Drive	C3	Craufurd Drive	B2	Mainsford Avenue	C3	Sinclairston Drive	C3
Barbieston Avenue	C3	Drumwhill Road	B3	Margaret Drain		Stair Drive	C4
Barbieston Cottages	A4	Farrell Crescent	B2	Crescent	B2	Station Court	C2
Bonnyton Avenue	C3	Garrowhill Drive	B3	Mill of Shield	A3, B3	Taiglum Place	B2
Burnbrae	C3	Glencraig Street	B3	Road		Torrance Drive	B2
Byres Road	A3	Hannahston Avenue	B3	Millmannoch	C3	Trabboch Avenue	B3
Cairnston Avenue	B3	Henry's Place	B1	Avenue		Truesdale Crescent	A3
Carston Drive	C3	Hodge Crescent	A3	Mull Gait	B2	Trysting Thorn	B2
Coal Road	C2	Ladies Walk	A3	Pettoch Road	A3	Wynd	
Coronation Road	B3, C3	Lane Crescent	B3	Reid Place	C2	Watson Terrace	A2
		Littlemill Road	C3	Robert Burns	B2	Whitegables Court	B2
		Lochmark Avenue	B3	Avenue		Woodend Cottages	C2

DALRY & DUNLOP

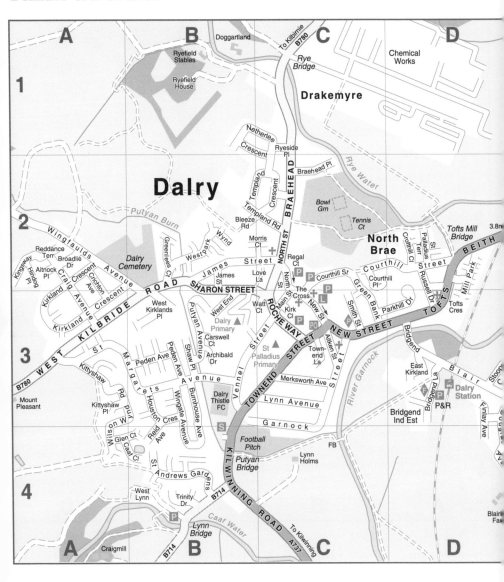

Doggartland
Ryefield Stables
Ryefield House
To Kilbirnie
B780
Rye Bridge

Chemical Works

Drakemyre

Netherlee Crescent
Ryeside Pl
Braehead Pl
Rye Water

Dalry

Templand Crescent
Templand Rd
BRAEHEAD

Bowl Grn
Tennis Ct

North Brae

Tofts Mill Bridge
3.8m

Putyan Burn
Bleeze Rd
Morris Ct
Street
NORTH ST
Regal Ct

Wingtaulds
Reddance Terr
Broadlie Dr
Kingsway
Aitnock Pl
Hindog Pl
Kirkland
Craig Avenue
Crescent
Crichton Ave
Kirkland Crescent
Avenue
Greenlees Ct
Dalry Cemetery
Westpark
Wynd
James Street
James St
Love La
Watt Ct

Palladius Terr
Crothill Cl
St
Russell Dr
Street
Courthill St
Courthill
Courthill Pl
Green Bank
BEITH
Mill Park

SHARON STREET
West End
West Kirklands Pl
Dalry Primary
Carswell Ct
Archibald Dr
ROCHEWAY
Kirk Cl
The Cross
New St
North St
Main St
Smith St
Parkhill Dr
TOFTS
Tofts Cres

WEST
B780
KILBRIDE ROAD
Kittyshaw Rd
St
Margarets
Peden Ave
Peden Ave
Shaw Pl
Putyan Avenue
Avenue
Burnhouse Ave
St Palladius Primary
Vennel
Street
TOWNEND STREET
Town-end La
Aitken St
NEW STREET
Bridgend
River Garnock

Mount Pleasant
Kittyshaw Pl
Willow Pl
Houston Cres
Wingate Avenue
Reid Ave
Dalry Thistle FC
Merksworth Ave
Lynn Avenue
Garnock
East Kirkland
Bridgend La
Dalry Station
P&R
Bridgend Ind Est

Glen Ct
Caaf Cl
St Andrews Gardens
KILWINNING ROAD
Football Pitch
Putyan Bridge
Lynn Holms
FB
Blair

West Lynn
Trinity Dr
B714
Caaf Water
Lynn Bridge
To Kilwinning
A737
Craigmill
B714

Finlay Ave
Stoorie
Blairlin Fa

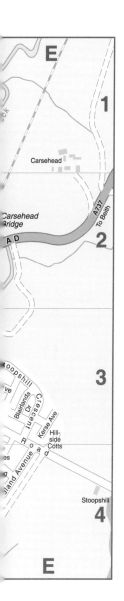

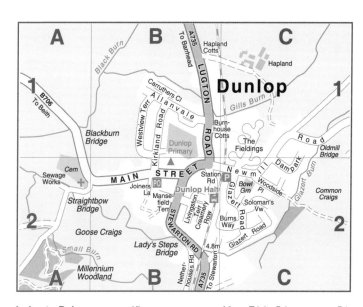

Index to Dalry

Aitken Street	C3	Kingsway	A2
Aitnock Place	A2	Kirk Close	C3
Archibald Drive	B3	Kirkland Crescent	A3
Beith Road	D2	Kittyshaw Place	A3
Blair Road	D3	Kittyshaw Road	A3
Blairlands Drive	E3	Love Lane	C2
Bleeze Road	B2	Lynn Avenue	C3
Braehead	C2	Main Street	C3
Braehead Place	C2	Mair Avenue	E3
Braidland Avenue	E4	Merksworth Avenue	C3
Bridgend	D3	Mill Park	D3
Bridgend Lane	D3	Morris Court	B2
Broadlie Drive	A2	Netherlee Crescent	B1
Burnhouse Avenue	B3	New Street	C3
Caaf Close	A4	North Street	C2
Carswell Court	B3	Parkhill Drive	C3
Cleeves Avenue	D4	Peden Avenue	B3
Courthill Place	C2	Putyan Avenue	B3
Courthill Street	C2	Reddance Terrace	A2
Craig Avenue	A2	Regal Court	C2
Crichton Avenue	A2	Reid Avenue	B4
Crofthill Close	D2	Roche Way	C3
Cross, The	C2	Russell Drive	D2
Douglas Avenue	D3	Ryefield House	B1
East Kirkland	D3	Ryeside Place	C1
Finlay Avenue	D3	St Andrews Gardens	B4
Garnock Street	C3	St Margarets Avenue	A3
Glen Court	A4	St Palladius Terrace	D2
Green Bank	C2	Sharon Street	B2
Greenlees Court	B2	Shaw Place	B3
Hillside Cottages	E3	Smith Street	C3
Hindog Place	A2	Stoopshill Crescent	D3
Houston Crescent	B3	Templand Crescent	B2
James Street	B2	Templand Road	B2
Kerse Avenue	E3	Tofts	D3
Kilwinning Road	B4	Tofts Crescent	D3
		Townend Lane	C3
		Townend Street	B3

Trinity Drive	B4
Vennel Street	B3
Watt Court	C3
West End	B3
West Kilbride Road	A3
West Kirklands Place	B3
West Lynn	B4
Westpark Wynd	B2
Wilson Wynd	A4
Wingate Avenue	B3
Wingfaulds Avenue	A2

Index to Dunlop

Allanvale	B1
Burnhouse Cottages	B1
Burns Way	C2
Carruthers Close	B1
Creamery Row	B2
Dampark	C2
Fieldings, The	C1
Glazert Road	C2
Hapland Cottages	B1
Joiners Lane	B2
Kirkland Road	B1
Livingston Terrace	B2
Lugton Road	B1
Main Street	B2
Mansefield Terrace	B2
Netherhouses Road	B2
New Mill Road	C2
Soloman's View	C2
Station Road	B2
Stewarton Road	B2
Westview Terrace	B1
Woodside Place	C2

DARVEL, DRYBRIDGE & DUNDONALD

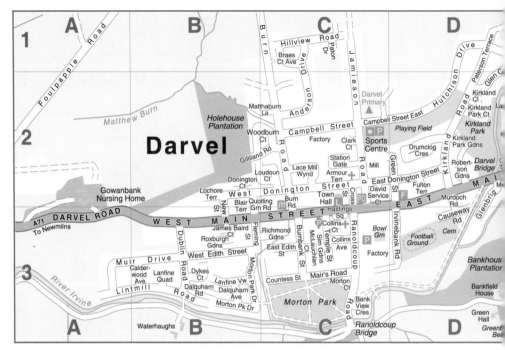

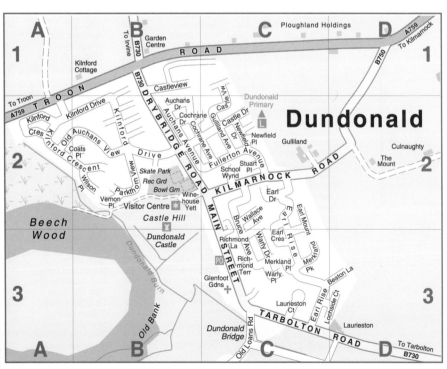

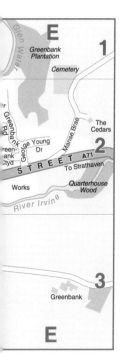

Index to Darvel

Anderson Drive	C2
Armour Terrace	C2
Bank View Crescent	C3
Blair Terrace	B2
Braes Court Avenue	C1
Burn Road	C1, C2
Burnbank Street	C3
Calderwood Avenue	B3
Campbell Street	C2
Campbell Street East	C2
Causeway Road	D3
Clark Court	C2
Collins Avenue	C3
Collins Court	C3
Countess Street	C3
Cross Street	C2
Dalquharn Avenue	B3
Dalquharn Road	B3
Darvel Road	A3
David Service Court	C2
Donington Court	B2
Drumclog Crescent	D2
Dublin Road	B3
Dykes Court	B3
East Donington Street	C2
East Edith Street	C3
East Main Street	D2
Fleming Street	B3
Foulpapple Road	A2
Fulton Road	D2
George Young Drive	E2
Gilliland Road	B2
Glen Crescent	D2
Glen Terrace	D2
Glenbrig	D3
Glenwater	D2
Green Street	D2
Greenbank Courtyard	E2
Greenbank Road	E2
Hastings Square	C3
Hillview Road	C1
Hutchison Drive	D2
Irvinebank Road	D3
James Baird Court	B3
Jamieson Road	C1
John Morton Crescent	D2
Kirkland Close	D2
Kirkland Park Court	D2
Kirkland Park Gardens	D2
Kirkland Road	D2
Lace Mill Wynd	C2
Laggan View	D2
Lanfine Quadrant	B3
Lanfine View	B3
Lintmill Road	A3
Lochore Terrace	B2
Loudoun Court	C2
McIlroy Court	D2
Mclauchlan Court	C3
Mair's Road	C3
Manse Brae	E2
Matthaburn Lane	B2
Morton Court	C3
Morton Park Drive	B3
Muir Drive	A3
Murdoch Road	D2
New Street	B2
Paterson Terrace	D2
Paton Drive	C1
Quoiting Green Road	B2
Ranoldcoup Road	C3
Richmond Gardens	C3
Robertson Gardens	D2
Roxburgh Gardens	B3
Sim Gardens	C3
Station Gate	C2
Temple Street	C3
West Donington Street	B2
West Edith Street	B3
West Main Street	B3
Woodburn Court	B2

Index to Dundonald

Auchans Avenue	B2
Auchans Drive	B2
Beaton Lane	D3
Bruce Avenue	C2
Castle Drive	C2
Castle View	C2
Castleview	B1
Coats Place	B2
Cochrane Avenue	B2
Cochrane Drive	B2
Drybridge Road	B2
Earl Crescent	C3
Earl Drive	C2
Earl Mount	C2
Earl Rise	C2, C3
Fullerton Avenue	C2
Glenfoot Gardens	C3
Gulliland Avenue	C2
Kilmarnock Road	C2
Kilnford Crescent	A2
Kilnford Drive	B2
Laurieston Court	C3
Lochside Court	C3
Main Street	C2
Merkland Park	C3
Merkland Place	C3
Newfield Drive	C2
Newfield Place	C2
Old Auchans View	A2
Old Loans Road	C3
Parkthorn View	B2
Richmond Lane	C3
Richmond Terrace	C3
School Wynd	C2
Stuart Place	C2
Tarbolton Road	C3
Troon Road	A2
Vernon Place	B2
Wallace Avenue	C2
Warly Drive	C3
Warly Place	C3
Wilson Place	B2
Winehouse Yett	B2

Index to Drybridge

Dreghorn Road	B1
Griers Walk	B2
Holms Farm Cottages	B1
Main Street	B2
Shewalton Drive	B2
Shewalton Moss	B2
Shewalton Road	A2
Station Row	C2

35

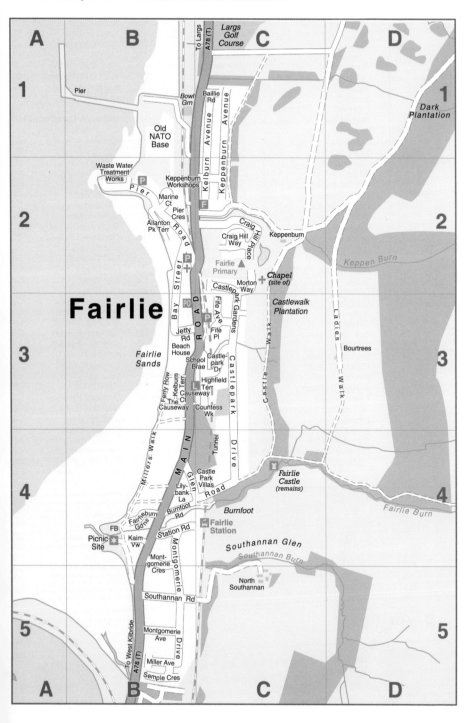

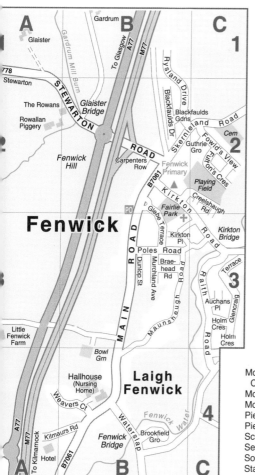

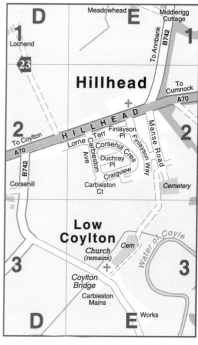

Montgomerie Crescent	B4	
Montgomerie Drive	B4	
Morton Way	C2	
Pier Crescent	B2	
Pier Road	B2	
School Brae	C3	
Semple Crescent	B5	
Southannan Road	B5	
Station Road	B4	

Kilmaurs Road	A4
Kirkton Place	B3
Kirkton Road	B2
Main Road	B3
Maunsheugh Road	B3
Murchland Avenue	B3
Poles Road	B3
Raith Road	C3
Rysland Drive	B1
Skernieland Road	B2
Stewarton Road	A2
Waterslap	B4
Weavers Court	B4

ex to Fairlie

ton Park Terrace	B2	
e Road	C1	
Street	B3	
h House	B3	
foot Road	B4	
e Walk	C3	
epark Drive	C3	
epark Gardens	C3	
epark Villas	C4	
eway Court	B3	
eway, The	B3	
tess Walk	C3	
Hill Place	C2	
Hill Way	C2	
eburne	B4	
dens		

Ferry Row	B3
Fife Avenue	C3
Fife Place	C3
Glen Road	B4
Highfield Terrace	C3
Jetty Road	B3
Kaim View	B4
Kelburn Avenue	C2
Kelburn Terrace	B3
Keppenburn Avenue	C2
Ladies Walk	D3
Lilybank Lane	B4
Main Road	B4
Marine Court	B2
Miller Avenue	B5
Millers Walk	B4
Montgomerie Avenue	B5

Index to Fenwick

Auchans Place	C3
Blackfaulds Drive	B2
Blackfaulds Gardens	B2
Braehead Road	B3
Brookfield Grove	B4
Carpenters Row	B2
Creelshaugh Road	C2
Dunlop Street	B3
Fowld's View	C2
Fulton's Crescent	C2
Glebe Terrace	B2
Glencraig Terrace	C3
Guthrie Grove	C2
Holm Crescent	C3

Index to Hillhead

Carbieston Avenue	E2
Carbieston Court	E2
Corsehill Crescent	E2
Craigview	E2
Duchray Place	E2
Finlayson Place	E2
Finlayson Way	E2
Hillhead	D2
Lorne Terrace	E2
Manse Road	E2

GALSTON & GIRVAN

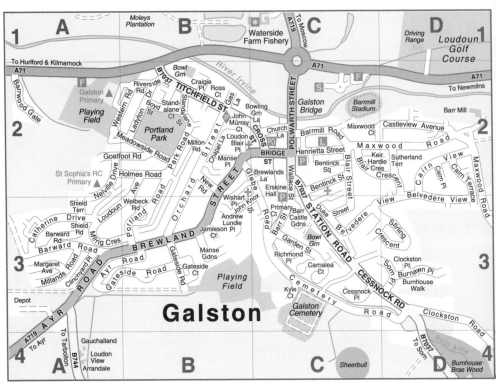

Index to Galston

Andrew Lundie Place	B3
Ayr Road	A3
Barr Castle Gardens	C3
Barr Street	C3
Barrmill Road	C2
Barward Road	A3
Barwood Gate	A2
Belvedere View	C3, D3
Bentinck Square	C2
Bentinck Street	C2
Blair Crescent	C2
Blair Street	C2
Bowling Green Lane	C2
Boyd Street	B2
Brewlands Lane	C2
Brewland Street	B3
Bridge Street	C2
Burnawn Place	D3
Burnhouse Walk	D3
Cairn Place	D2
Cairn Terrace	D2
Cairn View	D2
Carnalea Court	C3
Castleview Avenue	D2
Catherine Drive	A3
Cemetery Road	C3
Cessnock Place	C3
Cessnock Road	C3
Chapel Lane	B2
Church Lane	C2

Clinchyard Place	A3
Clockston Place	D3
Clockston Road	D3
Craigie Place	B2
Cross Street	C2
Duke Street	C3
Erskine Hall	C2
Garden Street	C3
Gas Lane	B2
Gateside Court	B3
Gateside Road	A3, B3
Glebe Road	B2
Goatfoot Road	A2
Henrietta Street	C2
Holmes Road	B2
Jamieson Court	B3
John Knox Street	B3
John Murray Court	B2
Keir Hardie Crescent	C2
Kyle Court	C3
Ladyton Drive	B2
Loudoun Avenue	A3
Loudoun Blair Place	B2
Manse Gardens	B3
Manse Place	B2
Margaret Avenue	A3
Maxwood Court	C2
Maxwood Road	D2
Meadowside Road	B2
Millands Road	A3
Milrig Crescent	A3
Milton Road	B2

Nelville Drive	A2
New Road	B2
Orchard Street	B3
Park Road	B2
Polwarth Street	C2
Portland Road	B3
Primary Court	C3
Richmond Place	C3
Riverside Road	B2
Ross Court	B2
Shield Road	A3
Shield Terrace	A3
Sorn Place	D3
Standalane Court	B2
Standalane Street	B2
Station Road	C3
Stirling Crescent	D3
Sutherland Terrace	D2
Titchfield Street	B2
Wallace Street	C2
Welbeck Road	B3
Western Road	A2
Wishart Place	B3

Index to Girvan

Ailsa Place	B3
Ailsa Street East	B3
Ailsa Street West	A3
Ainslie Road	A5
Ardmillan Road	C2
Arran Court	B4

Arran View	A2
Avenue, The	C3
Assel Place	C4
Ballochtoul	C4
Ballybroke Street	A4
Bay Terrace	A5
Beech Way	B5
Bennane Road	A5
Birch Terrace	B5
Bourtreehall	B2
Boyle Court	B2
Bridge Street	B2
Byne Cottages	B6
Byne Court	C4
Carrick Street	B2
Cauldshore	A5
Chalmers Arcade	B3
Chalmers Court (1)	B3
Cherry Drive	B5
Chestnut Drive	B4
Church Square	B2
Clyde View	C3
Coalpots Road	C4, B6
Connor Court	C3
Craig Court	B3
Cuddieston	C4
Dalrymple Street	B4
Deacons Place	B3
Doune Street	A4
Douneburn Crescent	A5
Downhill Road	B4
continued overleaf...

38

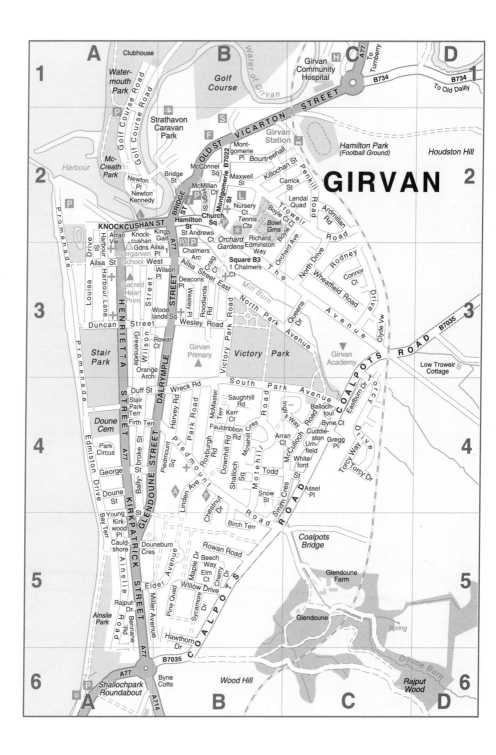

Girvan

A1 Clubhouse
Watermouth Park
Golf Course Road

B1 Golf Course
Water of Girvan

C1 Girvan Community Hospital
VICARTON STREET
A77 To Turnberry
B734

D1 B734
To Old Dailly

Strathavon Caravan Park
Girvan Station
OLD ST
Hamilton Park (Football Ground)
Houdston Hill

Harbour
McCreath Park
Montgomerie Pl
Bourtreehall
Newton Pl
Newton Kennedy
Bridge St
McConnel Sq
McMillan St
Maxwell St
Killochan St
Carrick St
Penkill Road
Ardmillian Road

GIRVAN 2

Lendal Quad
Troweir Road
Boyle Ct
Boyle
Bowl Grns
Orchard Ave
North Drive
The Avenue
Rodney
Connor Ct
Wheatfield Road

KNOCKCUSHAN ST
Arran Vw
Knockcushan Gdns
Kings Gait
Ailsa Pl
St Andrews Ct
Chalmers Arc
Richard St
Edminston Way
North Drive

Promenade
Louisa Drive
Ailsa St
Invergarven School
West
Wilson Pl
Ailsa Street East
Craig Ct
Square B3
1 Chalmers Ct
Orchard Ave
Clyde Vw

Sacred Heart Prim
Deacons Rd
Roodlands Rd
Wesley Pl
North Park Road
Mill Burn
Queens Dr

B7035 ROAD 3

Duncan Street
Greenside
Wesley Road
Rowan Ct
Girvan Primary
Victory Park
North Park Avenue
Girvan Academy

Low Troweir Cottage

Stair Park
Orange Arch
Union
DALRYMPLE STREET
South Park Avenue
COALPOTS ROAD

Promenade
Duff St
Stair Park Terr
Firth Terr
Wreck Rd
Hervey Rd
Park Road
McMaster Terr
Saughhill Rd
Kerr Ct
Inglis Way
Balloch-toul
Byne Ct
Torcy Way
Torcy Dr

Doune Cem
HENRIETTA STREET
Park Circus
Braboke St
Piedmount Sq
Fauldribbon Rd
Downhill Rd
Motehill Cres
Arran Ct
Cuddieston Urnfield
Whiteford
Gregg Pl

George St
Doune St
Linden Ave
Roxburgh Rd
Shalloch Sq
Motehill Road
Todd St
McCulloch Road
Snow St
Assel Pl

Young Kirkwood Pl
Cauldshore
Bay Terr
Chestnut Dr
Birch Terr
Smith Cres
Coalpots Bridge

KIRKPATRICK STREET
GLENDOUNE STREET
Ainslie Road
Douneburn Cres
Rowan Road
Beech Way
Elm Ct
Cherry Dr
Maple Dr
Glendoune Farm

Edmiston Drive
Elder Avenue
Willow Drive
Pine Quad
Sycamore Dr
COALPOTS ROAD

Spring
Glendoune

Rajput Dr
Bannane Rd
Miller Avenue
Hawthorn Dr

Ainslie Park
A77
B7035
Wood Hill
Rajput Wood

A6 Shallochpark Roundabout
Byne Cotts
A714

B6

C6

D6

39

HURLFORD & IRVINE

Index to Girvan
continued from overleaf...

Duff Street	A4
Duncan Street	A3
Eastburn Drive	C4
Edmiston Drive	A4
Elder Avenue	A5
Elm Court	B5
Fauldribbon Road	B4
Firth Terrace	A4
George Street	A4
Glendoune Street	A5
Golf Course Road	A2
Greenside	A3
Gregg Place	C4
Hamilton Street	B2
Harbour Lane	A3
Harbour Street	A3
Hawthorn Drive	B5
Henrietta Street	A3
Hervey Road	B4
High Street	B2
Inglis Way	C4
Kerr Court	B4
Killochan Street	B2
Kings Gait	B2
Kirkpatrick Street	A4
Kirkwood Place	A5
Knockcushan Gardens	A2
Knockcushan Street	A2
Lendal Quadrant	C2
Linden Avenue	B4
Louisa Drive	A3
McConnel Square	B2
McCulloch Road	C4
McMaster Terrace	B4
McMillan Court	B2

Maple Drive	B5
Maxwell Street	B2
Miller Avenue	A5
Montgomerie Place	B2
Montgomerie Street	B2
Motehill Crescent	B4
Motehill Road	B4
Newton Kennedy	A2
Newton Place	A2
North Drive	C3
North Park Avenue	B3
Nursery Court	B2
Old Street	B2
Orange Arch	A3
Orchard Avenue	B3
Park Circus	A4
Park Road	B4
Penkill Road	C2
Piedmount Road	B4
Piedmount Square	B4
Pine Quadrant	B5
Promenade	A3
Queens Drive	C3
Rajput Drive	A5
Richard Edminston Way	B3
Rodney Drive	C3
Roodlands Road	B3
Rowan Court	A3
Rowan Road	B5
Roxburgh Road	B4
St Andrews Court	B2
Saughhill Road	B4
Shalloch Square	B4
Smith Crescent	B4
Snow Street	B4
South Park Avenue	B4
Stair Park Terrace	A4

Sycamore Drive	B5
Todd Street	B4
Torcy Drive	C4
Torcy Way	C4
Troweir Road	B2
Urnfield	C4
Vicarton Street	B2
Victory Park Road	B3
Wesley Place	B3
Wesley Road	B3
Wheatfield Road	C3
Whiteford	C4
Willow Drive	B5
Wilson Place	B3
Wilson Street	A3
Woodlands Square	B3
Wreck Road	B4
Young Street	A5

Index to Hurlford

Academy Court	B3
Academy Street	B3
Ashton Drive	C4
Barleith Court	C4
Barnweil Drive	B4
Bellfield Avenue	A3
Bellfield Court	A3
Blair Avenue	B3, B4
Blair Crescent	B3
Blair Road	B3
Cessnock Avenue	C4
Cessnock Drive	C4
Cessnock Gardens	C3
Cessnock Road	C3

Craigie Road	C4
Cross,The	C3
Drumleyhill Drive	C4
Dykehead Drive	C4
Furnace Court	B3
Galston Road	C3
Graham Court	B3
Holyoake Court	C2
Kaimshill Cottages	A3
Kerrmuir Avenue	C4
Kersland Crescent	B3
Knowehead Road	C4
Leven Court	C3
Leven Drive	C3
Lifnock Avenue	C3
Lomond Avenue	C3
Main Road	B2
Marchmont Court	C2
Mauchline Road	C3
Maxwell Gardens	B3
Mayfield Avenue	D4
Morris Crescent	B3
Moss Court	C4
Ness Gardens	C3
Portland Brae	B2
Portland Court	B3
Reid Court	B2
Riccarton Mill Cottages	A3
Riccarton Road	A3
Richardson Avenue	D4
Roxburgh Road	B3
Salisbury Avenue	C2
Sherwood Road	C3
Station Drive	A3
Union Street	B3
Walden Road	B3
Walker Court	C3
Wallace Court	A3

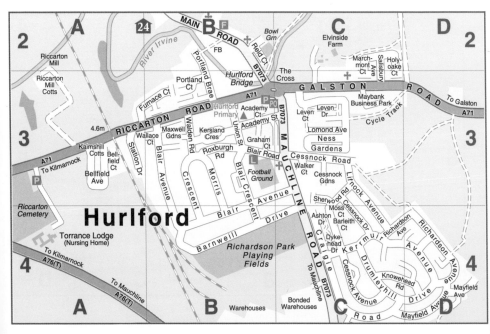

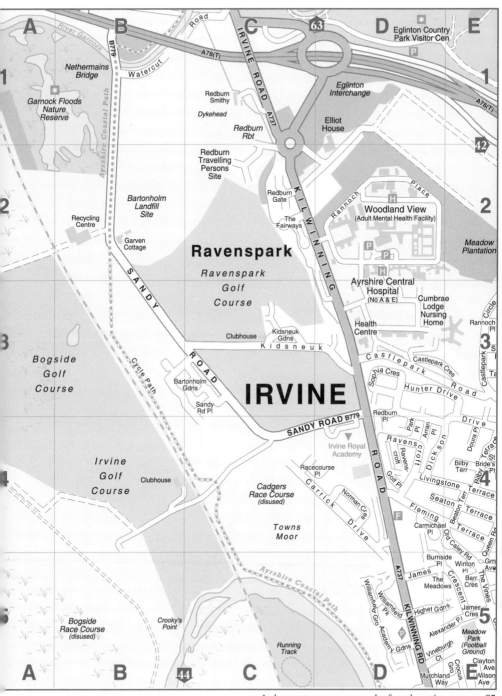

Index to street names can be found starting on page 97

IRVINE

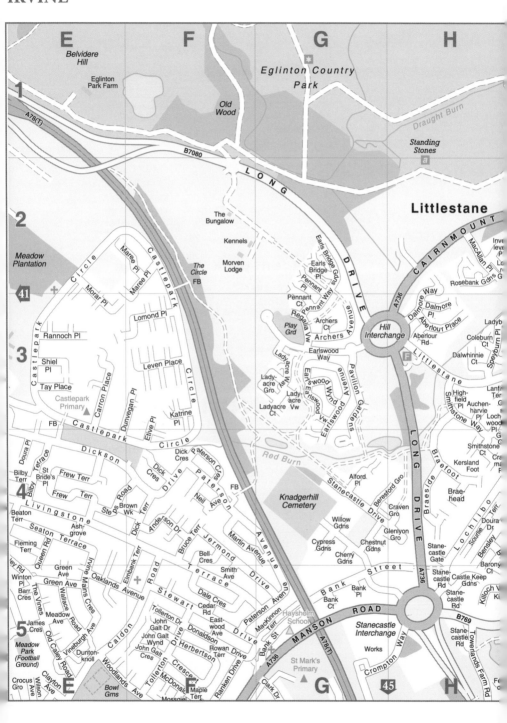

E   **F**   **G**   **H**

Belvidere Hill

Eglinton Park Farm

Eglinton Country Park

Old Wood

1

A78(T)

B7080

Standing Stones

Draught Burn

LONG

Littlestane

The Bungalow

Kennels

2

Meadow Plantation

The Circle

FB

Morven Lodge

Earls Bridge Gdns

Earls Bridge Pl

Pennant Way

Pennant Pl

CAIRNMOUNT

Inve leve P Lo G

Macallan Pl

Rosebank Gdns

A736

Circle

Maree Pl

Castlepark

Maree Pl

Morar Pl

Pennant Ct

Pennant Way

Regalia Vw

Way

Dalmore Pl

Aberlour Place

Ladyb

41

Lomond Pl

Play Grd

Archers Ct

Archers

Hill Interchange

Dalmore

Aberlour Rd

Coleburn Ct

Rannoch Pl

Leven Place

Earlswood Way

Earlswood

Pavilion Gardens

Dalwhinnie Ct

3

Shiel Pl

Castlepark

Carron Place

Circle

Ladyacre Way

Ladyacre Gro

Ladyacre Ct

Ladyacre Vw

Earlswood

Avenue

Littlestane

Highfield Pl

Auchenharvie Pl

Lanfi Ter G Loch wood Pl

Tay Place

Castlepark Primary

Katrine Pl

Etive Pl

Dunvegan Pl

Smithstone Way

Smithstone Ct

Kersland Foot

FB

Castlepark

Circle

Dick Cres

Paterson Cres

Red Burn

Alford Pl

LONG DRIVE

Braefoot

Cra ma F

4

Doura Pl

Dickson

Dick Cres

Paterson

FB

Knadgerhill Cemetery

Stanecastle Drive

Beresford Gro

Craven Gro

Braehead

Lochlibo

Doura Dr

Bilby Terr

St Bride's Pl

Frew Terr

Frew Terr

Dick Drive

Neil Ave

Anderson Dr

Willow Gdns

Glenlyon Gro

Sourlie Ct

Bensley

Beaton Terr

Livingstone

Ash-grove

Ste Brown Wk

Bruce Terr

Jermond Drive

Martin Avenue

Cypress Gdns

Chestnut Gdns

Stanecastle Gate

Barony Ct

Fleming Terr

Seaton Terrace

Irvine Mains Cres

Bell Cres

Smith Ave

Cherry Gdns

Stanecastle Castle Keep Gdns

Killoch V

ley Rd Winton Pl

Queen Rd

Green Ave

Elmbank Terr

Road

Terrace

Dale Cres

Bank Street

Bank Pl

Rd

Stanecastle Rd

Barr Cres

Green Ave

Oaklands Avenue

Stewart

Cedar Rd

Paterson Aven

Bank Ct

ROAD

B769

The Vines

Wallace Rd

Meadow Ave

Caldon

Tollerton Dr

East-wood Ave

MacKinnon Terr

Hayshelm School

Stanecastle Interchange

Stane-castle Rd

5

James Cres

Meadow Park (Football Ground)

Old Caley Road

Vineburgh Ave

Dunton-knoll

John Galt Dr

John Galt Wynd

John Galt Cres

Donaldson

D Herbertson

Rowan Terr

Rowan Drive

Bank St.

MANSON

A78(T)

A736

Works

Crompton Way

Stane-castle Rd

Crocus Gro

Wilson Ave

Clayton Ave

Woodlands Ave

Tollerton

McDonal

Crescent

Maple Terr

Ranken Drive

Clark Dr

St Mark's Primary

45

E   **F**   **G**   **H**

Bowl Grns

Mossgiel

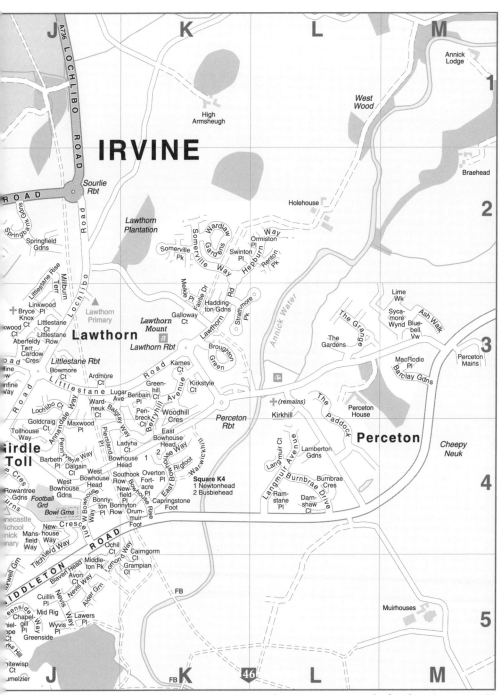

IRVINE

Index to street names can be found starting on page 97

IRVINE

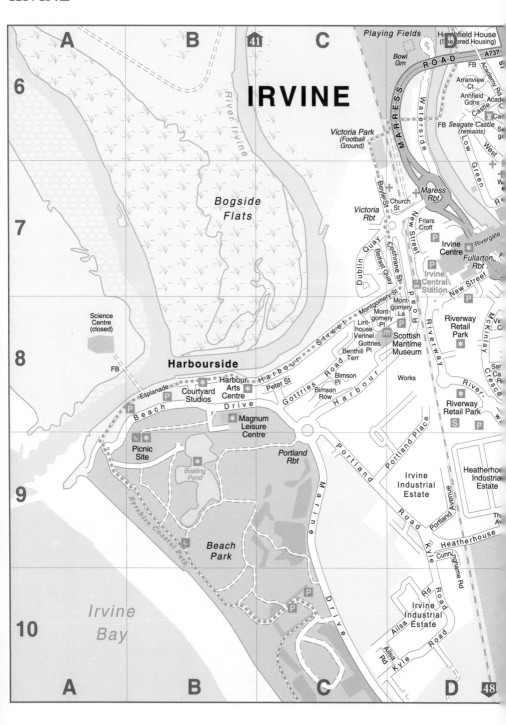

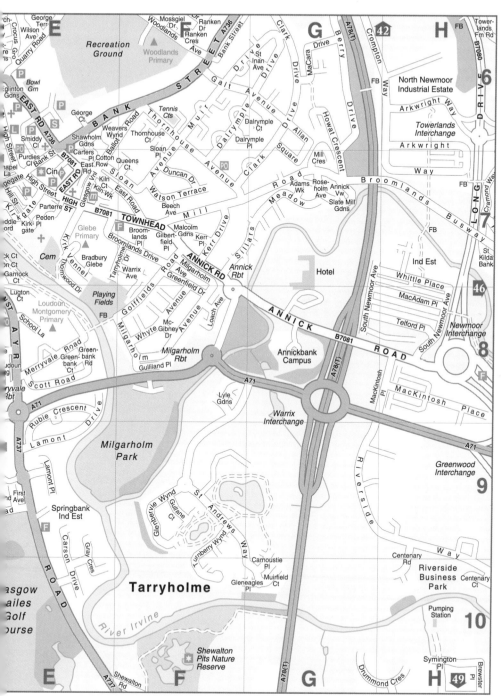

Index to street names can be found starting on page 97

IRVINE

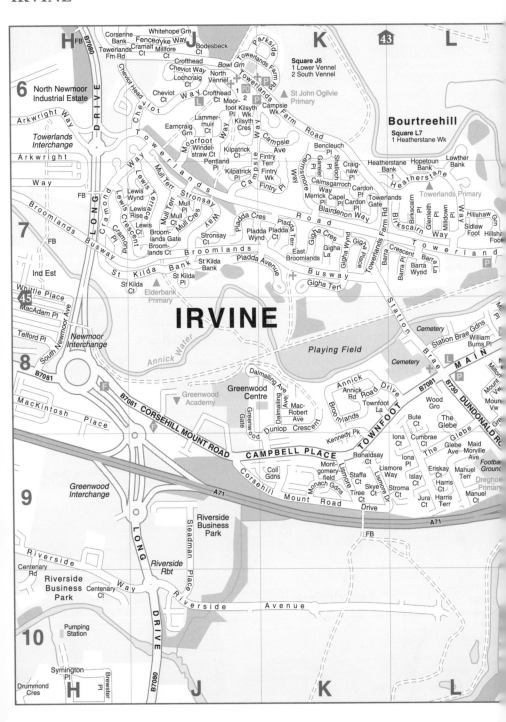

Square J6
1 Lower Vennel
2 South Vennel

St John Ogilvie Primary

Bourtreehill
Square L7
1 Heatherstane Wk

IRVINE

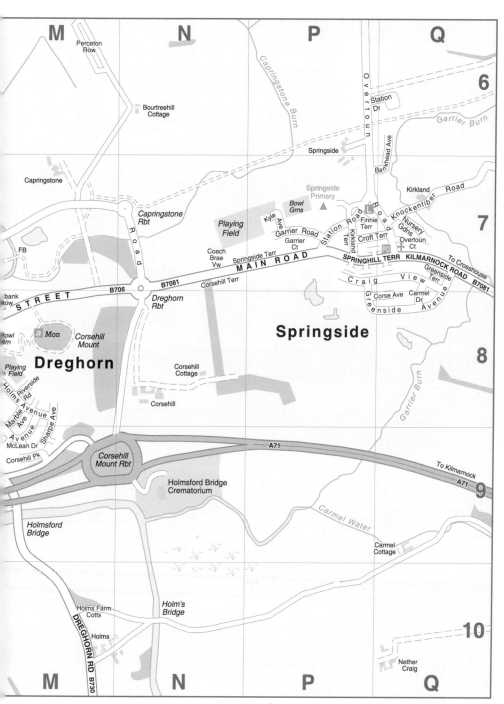

M · N · P · Q

Perceton Row

Bourtreehill Cottage

Capringstone Burn

Overtoun

Station Dr

6

Garrier Burn

Springside

Bankhead Ave

Capringstone

Capringstone Rbt

Kirkland Road

Springside Primary

Bowl Grns

Kyle Ave

Garrier Road

Road

Station Road

Finnie Terr

Kirkland Terr

Croft Terr

Nursery Gdns

Knockentiber Road

7

FB

Playing Field

Road

Coach Brae Vw

Garrier Ct

Springside Terr

MAIN ROAD

SPRINGHILL TERR

PO

Overtoun Ct

KILMARNOCK ROAD

To Crosshouse

B706

B7081

Corsehill Terr

Craig View

Greenside Terr

B7081

bank low

STREET

Dreghorn Rbt

Corse Ave

Carmel Dr

Greenside Avenue

Springside

Bowl rn

Mon

Corsehill Mount

Dreghorn

8

Corsehill Cottage

Garrier Burn

Playing Field

Holms Riverside Rd

Corsehill

Marble Ave

Holms Avenue

Sharpe Ave

Avenue

McLean Dr

Corsehill Pk

A71

Corsehill Mount Rbt

To Kilmarnock

A71

9

Holmsford Bridge Crematorium

Holmsford Bridge

Carmel Water

Carmel Cottage

Holms Farm Cotts

Holm's Bridge

DREGHORN RD

Holms

B730

10

Nether Craig

M · N · P · Q

Index to street names can be found starting on page 97

47

IRVINE

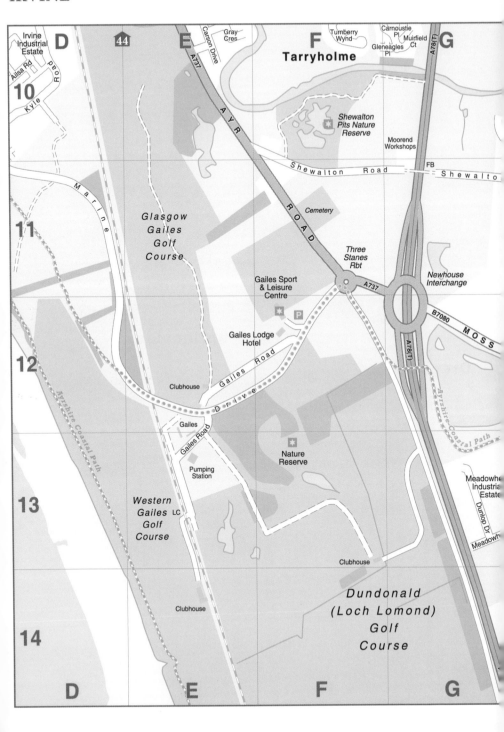

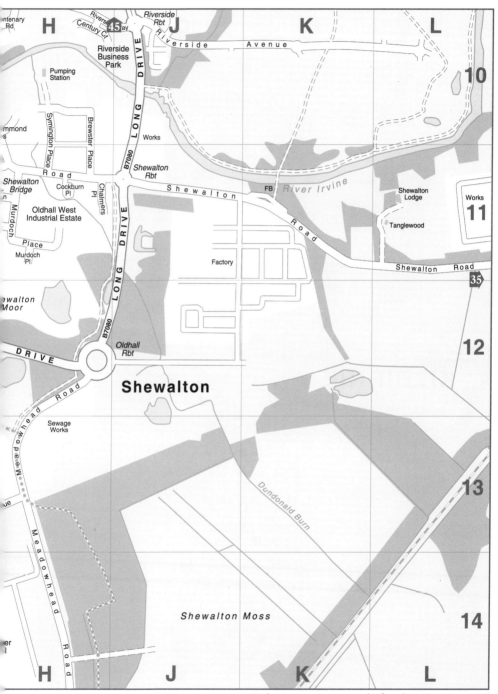

Index to street names can be found starting on page 97

49

KILBIRNIE

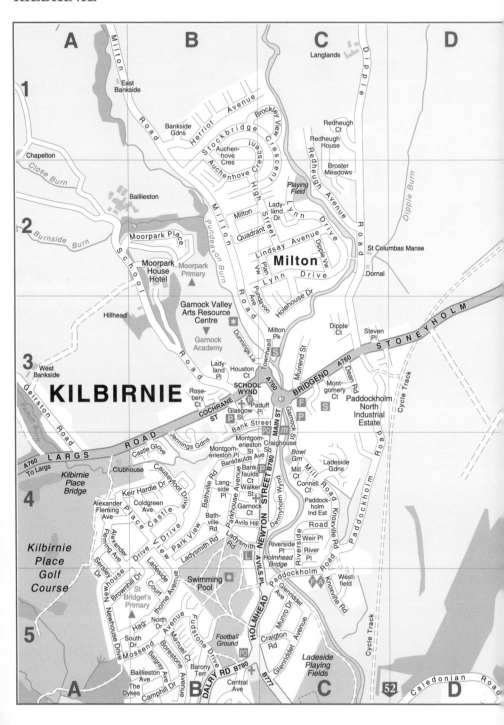

A   **B**   **C**   **D**

Langlands

East Bankside

Chapelton

Close Burn

Baillieston

Burnside Burn

Moorpark Place

Moorpark House Hotel

Moorpark Primary

Hillhead

West Bankside

Geirston Road

Paduff Burn

A760 To Largs

LARGS

KILBIRNIE

ROAD

COCHRANE ST

Rosebery Ct

Glasgow St

Bank Street

SCHOOL WYND

Jennings Gdns

Castle Grove

Clubhouse

Kilbirnie Place Bridge

Keir Hardie Dr

Causeyfoot Drive

Castle Grove

Alexander Fleming Ave

Coldgreen Ave

Castle Drive

Park View

Ladeside

Alexander Fleming Ave

Sersley Dr

Newhouse Drive

Brownhill Dr

Court

St Bridget's Primary

Hag'

North Dr

South Dr

Mossend

Baillieston Ave

The Dykes

Camphill Dr

thorne Avenue

Manuel Ct

Borestone Avenue

Balgray Ave

Barony Terr

Kilbirnie Place Golf Course

Milton Road

Herriot Avenue

Bankside Gdns

Stockbridge

Auchenhove Cres

Auchenhove Cres

High Street

Milton

Quadrant

Brockley View

Crescent

School Road

Pundeavon Burn

Milton Road

Garnock Valley Arts Resource Centre

Garnock Academy

Dunnings La

Ladyland Pl

Houston Ct

Paduff Pl

Montgomerieston St

Montgomerieston Ave

Bankfaulds

Langside Pl

Bathville

Parkhouse

Garnock Ct

Bathville Rd

Ladysmith Rd

Ladeside

Fudstone Drive

Football Ground

Swimming Pool

Central Ave

DALRY RD B780

Ladyland Dr

Milton

Lindsay Avenue

Lynn Drive

Holehouse Dr

Milton Pk

Townhead

Pundeavon Ave

Playing Field

Milton

Lynn Drive

Dipple Vw

Dipple Vw

Pundeavon Ave

Dipple Ct

Dipple

Steven Pl

Mulrend St

BRIDGEND

A760

MAIN ST

Garnock St

Craighouse

Montgomerieston Sq

Bankfaulds Ct

Walker St

Avils Hill

NEWTON STREET B780

Dennyholm Wynd

Riverside Pl

River Pl

Holmhead Bridge

Paddockholm

Glenriddet Ave

Munro Dr

Craigton Rd

Glenriddet Avenue

B771

Bowl Grn

Mill Ct

Connell St

Paddockholm Ind Est

Road

Weir Pl

West-field

Redheugh Ct

Redheugh House

Broster Meadows

Redheugh Avenue

St Columbas Manse

Dornal

Dipple Burn

Dipple

STONEYHOLM

Mont- gomery Ct

Dean Rd

Paddockholm North Industrial Estate

Ladeside Gdns

Mill Road

Knoxville Rd

Knoxville Rd

Paddockholm Road

Cycle Track

Cycle Track

Ladeside Playing Fields

Caledonian Road

52

50

Index to Kilbirnie

Alexander Fleming Avenue	A4
Auchengree Road	E7
Auchenhove Crescent	B1, B2
Avils Hill	B4
Avils Place	C5
Baillieston Avenue	B5
Balgray Avenue	B5
Balgray Road	C6
Bank Street	B3
Bankfaulds Avenue	B4
Bankfaulds Court	B4
Bankside Gardens	C1
Barony Terrace	B5, B6
Bathville Road	B4
Beith Road	D7
Borestone Avenue	B5, B6
Bridgend	C3
Briery Court	B6
Brockley View	B1
Broster Meadows	C1
Brownhill Drive	A5
Burnside Street	C7
Caledonian Place	C6
Caledonian Road	D5, C6
Camphill Drive	B5
Castle Drive	B4
Castle Grove	B4
Causeyfoot Drive	B4
Central Avenue	B5, B6
Cochrane Street	B3
Coldgreen Avenue	B4
Connell Court	C4
Craigends Road	C7
Craighouse Square	C4
Craigton Road	C5
Daisybank	D7
Dalry Road	A7, B5
Davidson Avenue	E7
Dean Road	C3
Dennyholm Wynd	C4
Dipple Court	C3
Dipple Road	C2
Dipple View	C2
Dunnings Lane	B3
Dykes, The	B5
Eastern Crescent	B6
Fudstone Drive	B5
Garnock Court	B4
Garnock Street	C3
Garnock View	C6
Garnockside	C7
Geirston Road	A3
Glasgow Street	B3
Glebe Road	C6
Glenriddet Avenue	C5
Grahamston Avenue	C6
Greenside Avenue	B6
Hagthorne Avenue	B5
Herriot Avenue	B1
High Street	C2
Holehouse Drive	C3
Holmhead	B5
Holms Road	C7
Houston Court	B3
Jennings Gardens	B4
Keir Hardie Drive	B4
Kersland Place	D7
Kersland Road	D7
Kerswinning Avenue	B6
Kirkland Road	C6
Knoxville Road	C4, C5
Ladeside Court	B4
Ladeside Gardens	C4
Ladyland Drive	C2
Ladyland Place	B3
Ladysmith Road	B4
Langside Place	B4
Largs Road	A4
Lindsay Avenue	C2
Loadingbank Court	B6
Loadingbank	B6
Lochend Road	D6
Longbar Avenue	E7
Lynn Drive	C2
Main Road	C7
Main Street	C4
Manuel Court	B5
Mill Court	C4
Mill Road	C4
Milton Park	C3
Milton Quadrant	B2
Milton Road	B2
Montgomerieston Place	B4
Montgomerieston Street	B4
Montgomery Court	C3
Moorpark Place	B2
Mossend Avenue	B5
Muirend Street	C3
Munro Drive	C5
Newhouse Drive	A5
Newton Street	C4
North Drive	B5
Paddockholm Road	C5
Paduff Place	B3
Park View	B4
Parkhouse Avenue	B4
Place View	B4
Plan View	C2
Pundavon Avenue	B2
Redheugh Avenue	C1
Redheugh Court	C1
Redheugh House	C1
River Place	C4
Riverside Place	C4
Riverside Road	C4
Rosebery Court	B3
St Brennans Court	B6
School Road	A2
School Wynd	B3
Sersley Drive	A4
Smith Avenue	E7
South Drive	B5
South Neuk	B6
Station Court	D7
Steven Place	C3
Stockbridge Crescent	B1
Stoneyholm Road	C3
Sunderland Court	B6
Townhead	C3
Walker Street	B4
Weir Place	C4
Western Crescent	B6
Westfield	C5
Willowburn Road	G6
Willowyard Road	G5

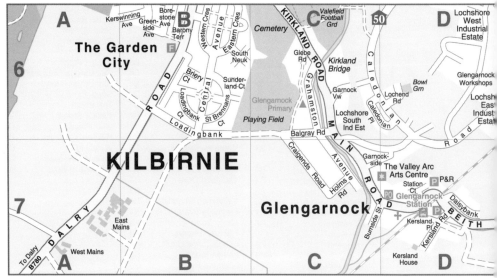

Index to street names in Kilbirnie can be found on page 51

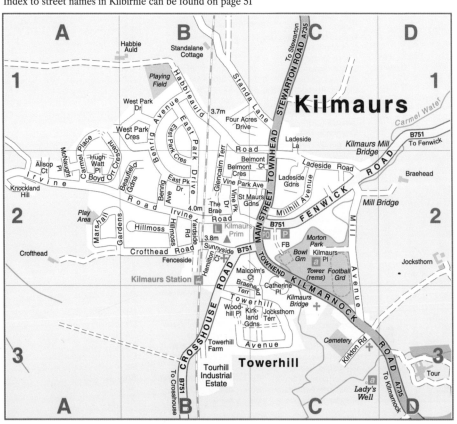

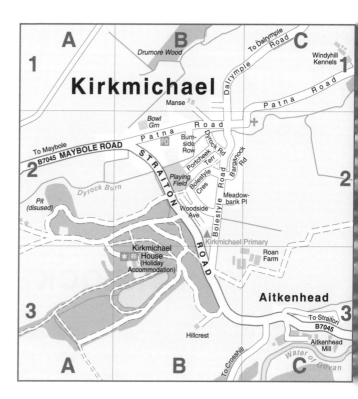

dex to Kilmaurs

sop Court	A2
aufield Gardens	B2
lmont Court	C2
lmont Crescent	C2
nrig Avenue	B2
yd Orr Crescent	A2
ae, The	B2
aehead Terrace	B2
rmel Place	A2
therine Place	C2
ofthead Road	B2
osshouse Road	B3
st Park Crescent	B1
st Park Drive	B1
nwick Road	C2
ar Acres Drive	B1
encairn Terrace	B2
obieauld Road	B1
milton Court	B2
moss	B2
gh Watt Place	A2

Irvine Road	A2, B2
Jocksthorn Terrace	C3
Kilmarnock Road	C2
Kilmaurs Place	C2
Kirkland Gardens	B3
Kirkton Road	C3
Knockland Hill	A2
Ladeside Gardens	C2
Ladeside Lane	C1
Ladeside Road	C2
McNaught Place	A2
Main Street	C2
Malcolm's Court	C2
Marshall Gardens	A2
Mill Avenue	C2
Millhill Avenue	C2
St Maurs Gardens	B2
Standa Lane	B1
Stewarton Road	C1
Sunnyside	B2
Towerhill Avenue	B3
Townend	C2
Townhead	C2

Vine Park Avenue	B2
Vine Park Drive	B2
West Park Crescent	B1
West Park Drive	B1
Woodhill Place	B3
Yardside Road	B2

Index to Kirkmichael

Barganock Road	B2
Bolestyle Crescent	B2
Bolestyle Road	B2
Burnside Row	B2
Dalrymple Road	B1
Dyrock Road	B2
Maybole Road	A2
Meadowbank Place	B2
Patna Road	B2
Portcheek Terrace	B2
Straiton Road	B2
Woodside Avenue	B2

KILMARNOCK

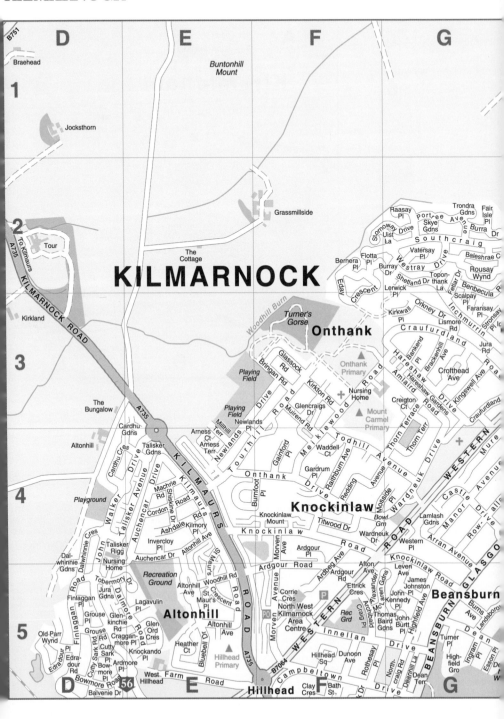

KILMARNOCK

Onthank

Knockinlaw

Altonhill

Beansburn

Hillhead

Map labels

H   J   K

Meiklewood

B7038

ROAD

A77 To Glasgow

1

Southcraig Holdings

Northcraig Cottage

Res (covered)

The Sheiling

Rowallan Business Park

P

Craighall Cres

Craighall

Meiklewood Belt

Craighall Bank

Craighall Bank

Lochranza Ct

Dunollie Gdns   Lochmaben Wynd   Ochiltree Pl   Rumford Pl

Dunskey Road   Lauriston Way   Porting Cross   Auchen-tiber Pl

unure Pl   Dun-donald Ct   Newmilns Gdns   Tarbolton Pl   Boydston Way

Priest-land Cl   Darvel   Mauchline Cres   Stewarton Ave   Dalgarven Ms   Crosshill Wynd

Colonsay Pl   Ave   Galston Pl   Lugar   Fenwick Cl   Southcraig Holdings

nda   Bressay   Wynd   Kingsford Pl   West-field Rd   Holly-bush Pl

ay   Cumbrae Drive   Rona   Hestan Pl   Burns Way   Burns Cres

skay   Harris Pl

Allsa Pl   Davaar   S   F   B7038   De Walden Drive

Lewis Dr   ROAD   B7064

AVENUE   Grougar Dr   Forest Grove   Wardneuk Plantation

ilford   Grougar Gdns   Assloss Grove   Riding School

wallan   Woodlands Grove   Assloss Road   Assloss Mains

Assloss Bridge

Hollybrae Plantation

Dean Castle Country Park

Dean Castle (restored)   Judas Hill Plantation

Dean Bridge

tor   Culloden Pl   Glenlivet Pl

Lauder Bridge   Otterburn Ave   South Dean Plantation

Bannock-burn Pl   Largs Avenue

H   Drumclog Pl   57   Kennedy Ct   Russell Ct   Skene Rd   Cameron Dr   Barclay Dr   J   Huntly Pl   GRASSYARDS

Fenwick Water

Borland House

Borland Bridge

Broombrae

2

Clark's Wood

3

Assloss

Assloss Cottage

FB

Parkers Mount

Wardlaw Plantation

Craufurdland Water

Dean View

Willie Ross Pl   Angus Ct   Niven Ct   Drive

Grassyards Interchange

Kennedy   Duncan Ct   Sinclair Ct   Balfour Ct

Maxwell Ct

Target Plantation   Silverwood ▲ Primary

Living-stone Ct   Rankin   Finlayson Dr   Lindsay Gdns   Donaldson Rd

Huntly   Lauder Ct   Donald-son Dr

Cameron Dr   Lindsay Pl   Cliff Ct   Walk   Wk

ROAD   B7082

Whinpark

4

5

Sutherland

K

Index to Kilmarnock

Aberfeldy Place	B8
Academy Apartments	G8
Academy Street	F10
Afton Avenue	F5
Ailsa Place	H3
Aird Avenue	E9
Alder Place	D8
Alexander McLaren Gardens	F5
Alloway Avenue	H8
Almond Place	D8
Altonhill Avenue	E5
Amlaird Road	G3
Anderson Place	K6
Angus Court	K4
Annan Court	G11
Annan Road	G11
Annanhill Avenue	C7
Annanhill House	C8
Annick Place	G11
Arbuckle Street	G8
Archibald Craig Place	F5
Ardbeg Avenue	F5
Ardgour Place	F4
Ardgour Road	F5
Ardle Avenue	H11
Ardmore Place	D5
Armour Street	F9
Armstrong Road	J6
Arness Court	E4
Arness Terrace	E4
Arran Avenue	G4
Arrothill Drive	D9
Ash Place	D9
Ashdale Road	E4
Assloss Road	H4, J4
Auchencar Drive	E4
Auchentiber Place	J2
Avon Place	H11
Ayr Road	E13
Bailiehill Place	D7
Baird Place	H6
Baird Road	H6
Baleshrae Crescent	G2
Balfour Court	K5
Balgray Avenue	F14
Ballochmyle Walk	B9
Balmoral Road	E6
Balvenie Drive	D5, D6
Bank Place	F8
Bank Street	F8
Bankend Place	G3
Bannerman Drive	K6
Bannockburn Place	H5
Barassie Place	E12
Barbadoes Place	E10
Barbadoes Road	E10
Barclay Drive	J5, J6
Barnweil Road	E11
Bath Street	F5, F6
Beansburn	G5
Beauly Crescent	G11
Beech Avenue	D8
Belleisle Place	E12
Bellevue Gardens	D7
Bellevue Road	D7
Bellfield Avenue	K10
Bellfield Court	K10
Bellsland Drive	F10
Bellsland Grove	F10
Bellsland Place	G9
Benbecula Road	G2
Bentinck Street	F9
Bernera Place	F2
Birch Place	D8
Blacksyke Avenue	E13
Blackwood Avenue	D9
Blair Street	F6
Bluebell Drive	E5

continued on page 58...

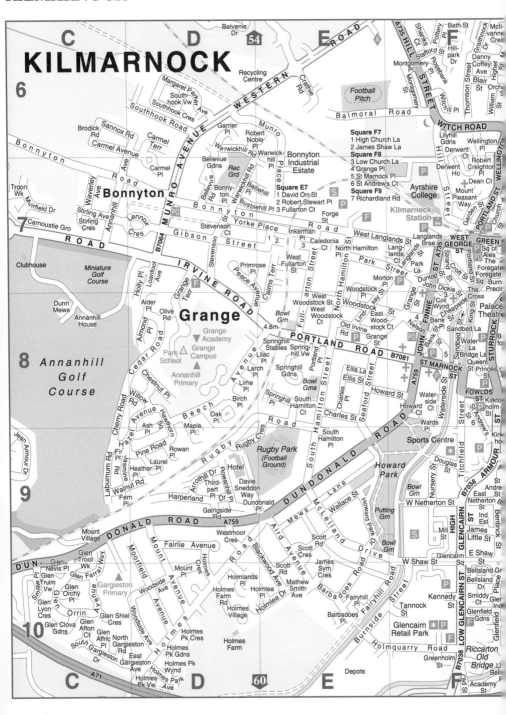

KILMARNOCK

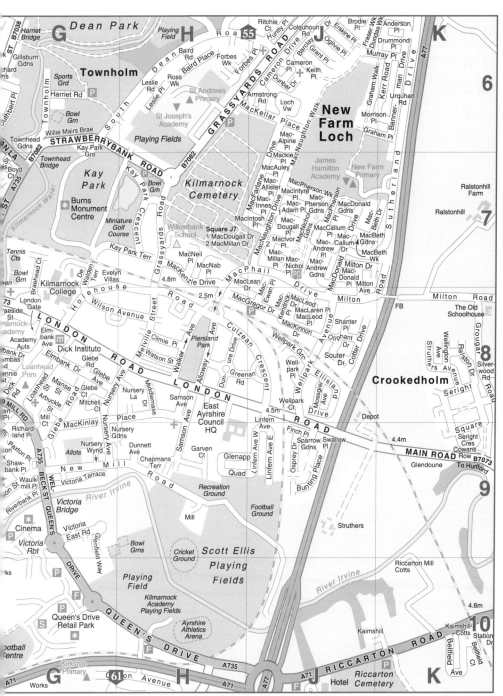

Index to street names can be found on pages 55 and 58-61

KILMARNOCK

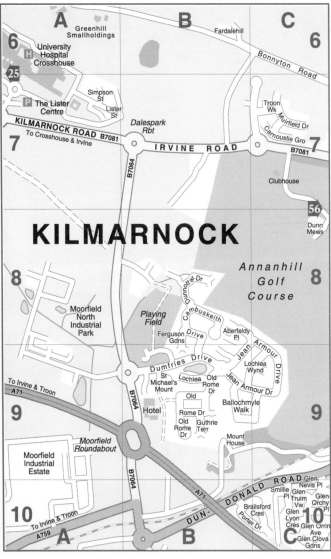

Cardhu Gardens	
Carmel Avenue	
Carmel Place	
Carmel Terrace	
Carnoustie Grove	
Carron Avenue	G10, G
Castle Drive	
Cedar Road	
Central Avenue	F
Cessock Place	H
Chapmans Terrace	
Charles Place	
Charles Street	
Cheapside Street	
Cherry Road	
Chestnut Place	
Cheviot Place	G
Church Lane	
Church Street	
Clark Street	
Clay Crescent	
Clayslaps View	H
Climie Place	
Clyde Place	G
College Wynd	
Colonsay Place	
Colquhoun Road	
Columbas Wynd	
Commonhead Road	
Cordon Road	
Corrie Crescent	
Cotter Drive	
Cowans Row	
Cragganmore Place	
Craighall Bank	
Craighall Crescent	
Craighall Road	
Craigie Avenue	
Craigie Place	
Craigie Road	F12,
Crathie Road	
Craufurdland Road	
Creigton Court	
Criffel Place	
Croe Place	
Croft Street	
Crofthead Avenue	
Cromdale Road	
Cross, The	
Crosshill Wynd	
Cruachan Place	
Cuillin Place	
Culloden Place	
Culzean Crescent	
Cumbrae Drive	
Cunninghame Drive	
Cuthbert Place	
Cutty Sark Place	
Cutty Sark Road	
Dalgarven Mews	
Dalmore Road	
Dalwhinnie Crescent	
Dalwhinnie Gardens	
Damhead Road	
Danny Coffey Avenue	
Darnley Drive	
Darvel Avenue	
Davaar Drive	
David Orr Street (1)	
Davie Sneddon Way	
De Walden Drive	
De Walden Terrace	
Dean Court	
Dean Lane	
Dean Road	
Dean Street	
Dean Terrace	
Dean View	
Deanhill Lane	
Dee Avenue	
Denholm Way	
Derwent Court	

continued from page 55...

Bonnyton Place	D7	Bringan Road	F3	Burra Drive	G2
Bonnyton Road	C6, D7	Brodick Road	C6	Burray Drive	G2
Bowmore Place	D5	Brodie Place	J6	Busbiehill Place	D7
Bowmore Road	D5	Broom Place	H11	Cairngorm Road	H13
Boyd Court	G7	Broomhill Quadrant	G12	Cairns Terrace	E7
Boyd Street	G7	Broomhill Road East	G12	Calder Place	G11
Boydston Way	J2	Broomhill Road West	F12	Caledonia Court	E7
Brackenhill Avenue	G3	Bruce Crescent	F12	Cambuskeith Drive	B8
Braefoot	F8	Bruce Street	F12	Cameron Drive	J5, J6
Braehead Court	G8	Buchanan Place	G11	Cameron Place	J6
Braeside Street	G8	Bunting Place	J9	Campbell Place	F11
Brailsford Crescent	B10	Burnfoot Place	E4	Campbell Street	F11
Bressay Place	H3	Burnpark Road	F13	Campbeltown Drive	F5
Brewery Road	F9	Burns Avenue	G5	Campsie Road	G13
Bridge Lane	F8	Burns Crescent	H3	Caprington	E13, F13
Bridgehouse Court	G14	Burns Precinct	F7	Avenue	
Bridgehousehill Road	F14	Burns Way	H3	Caprington Gardens	E13
		Burnside Street	E10	Cardhu Crescent	D4

went House	F7	Fulton's Lane	F7	Holly Place	D7	Landsborough Drive	G5
eron Road	G11	Gailes Place	E12	Hollybush Place	H2	Langcraig Road	F14
k Road	G8	Gainford Place	F4	Holmes Crescent	D9	Langlands Brae	F7
on Drive	E12	Gallion Walk	F9	Holmes Farm Road	D10	Langlands Court	F7
aldson Drive	K5	Galrigside Road	D9	Holmes Park Avenue	D10	Langlands Street	F7
aldson Road	K5	Galston Place	H2	Holmes Park Crescent	D10	Langside Avenue	F14
in Place	H12	Garden Street	F7	Holmes Park Gardens	D10	Laputa Place	E13
glas Street	F9	Gardrum Place	F4	Holmes Park View	D10	Larch Place	D8
nclog Place	H5	Garnock Road	G11	Holmes Park Wynd	D10	Largs Avenue	H5
mmond Place	K6	Garrier Place	D6	Holmes Road	D10	Lauder Court	J5
Place	J5	Garry Place	G11	Holmes Village	D10	Laurel Place	D9
nfries Drive	B9	Garven Court	H9	Holmlands Place	D10	Lauriston Way	H2
ngoyne Road	G13	Gateside Place	F12	Holmlea Drive	E10	Lawers Crescent	G12
bar Drive	J6	Gibson Street	D7	Holmlea Place	D10	Lawers Road	G12
can Court	K4	Gillsburn Gardens	G6	Holmquarry Road	E10	Lawson Street	G9
das Walk	J6	Gilmour Street	F9	Howard Court	F8	Leadhills Road	G13
donald Court	H2	Glasgow Road	G5, J3	Howard Park Drive	E9	Lennox Crescent	D7
donald Place	E9	Glassock Road	F3	Howard Street	E8	Lerwick Place	G2
donald Road	B10, E9	Glebe Avenue	G8	Huntly Court	J5	Leslie Place	H6
gavel Road	G12	Glebe Court	G8	Huntly Place	J5	Leslie Road	H6
lop Street	F7	Glebe Road	G9	Hurlford Road	F11, G11	Leven Avenue	G5
n Mews	C8	Glen Affric Place	C10	Inchgotrick Road	E12	Lewis Drive	H3
nett Avenue	H9	Glen Afton Court	C10	Inchmurrin Drive	G3	Lilac Place	E8
nottar Drive	B8	Glen Clova Gardens	C10	Ingram Place	G5	Lilyhill Gardens	F6
ollie Gardens	H2	Glen Farrar Way	C10	Inkerman Place	E7	Lime Place	D8
oon Avenue	F5	Glen Lyon Crescent	C10	Innellan Drive	F5	Lindsay Drive	J5
skey Road	H2	Glen Nevis Place	C10	Invercloy Place	E4	Lindsay Gardens	K5
ure Drive	H8	Glen Orchy Place	C10	Iona Place	G3	Lindsay Street	E8
ure Place	H2	Glen Ord Crescent	E5	Irvine Road	B7	Linfern Avenue East	J9
ston Avenue	F13	Glen Orrin Avenue	C10	Islay Place	H3	Linfern Avenue West	J9
Place	H11	Glen Shiel Crescent	C10	James Johnston Place	G5	Linfern Avenue	J8
Gargieston	D10	Glen Trool Walk	C9	James Little Street	F9	Lismore Road	G3
nue		Glen Truim View	C10	James Shaw Lane (2)	F7	Lister Street	A7
Netherton Street	F9	Glenapp Quadrant	H9	James Sym Crescent	E10	Little Bellsland Road	F10
Shaw Street	F9	Glencairn Square	F9	Jasmine Road	C9	Livingstone Court	J5
Woodstock Court	E8	Glencraigs Drive	F3	Jean Armour Drive	B9, C9	Loanfoot Avenue	D7
Crescent	F2	Glendoune	K9	Jeffrey Street	F11	Loanhead Street	G8
Place	H11	Glenfield Gardens	F10	John Burtt Place	G5	Loch View	J6
dour Place	D5	Glenfield Place	F10	John Dickie Street	F7	Lochgreen Place	E12
dour Road	D5	Glenfield Way	G9	John Finnie Street	F8	Lochlea	B9
rslie Crescent	E12	Glenkinchie Road	D5	John Kennedy Place	G5	Lochlea Wynd	B9
Lane	E8	Glenlivet Place	H5	John Walker Drive	D4	Lochmaben Wynd	H2
Street	E8	Graham Place	J6	Jura Gardens	D5	Lochnagar Road	G12
and Drive	J8	Graham Walk	J6	Jura Road	G3	Lochranza Court	H2
ank Avenue	G8	Graithnock Drive	F6	Kaimshill	J10	Lomond Road	G12
ank Drive	G8	Grampian Road	H13	Kaimshill Cottages	K10	London Gate	G8
ay Place	H3	Grange Place (4)	F8	Katrine Court	G11	London Road	G8
ne Place	J6	Grange Street	E8, F8	Kay Park Crescent	H7	Loreny Drive	E13, E14
Road	H12	Grange Terrace	D7	Kay Park Grove	G6	Loudoun Avenue	G12
n Place	G5	Granger Road	E11	Kay Park Terrace	G7	Low Church Lane (3)	F8
k Crescent	F5	Grant Place	J6	Keith Place	J6	Low Glencairn Street	F10
rn Villas	G7	Grassyards Road	H6, H7	Kelburn Crescent	E12	Lowther Place	G12
rd Place	H3	Green Street	F7	Ken Road	G11	Luce Avenue	G11
sle Place	G2	Greenan Road	H8	Kennedy Court	J5	Lugar Wynd	H2
e Avenue	D9	Greenholm Street	F10	Kennedy Drive	J5-K5	MacAdam Place	J7
nill Place	E10	Grougar Drive	H3	Kennedy Street	F10	MacAllister Place	J7
hill Road	E10	Grougar Gardens	H4	Kerr Road	K6	MacAlpine Place	J6
nsay Place	G3	Grougar Road	K8	Kilmarnock Road	A7	MacAndrew Gardens	J7
alehill	B6	Grouse Place	D5	(Crosshouse)		MacAndrew Place	J7
Road	E5	Grouse Road	D5	Kilmarnock Road	D2	MacAuley Place	J7
ick Close	H2	Guthrie Terrace	B9	(Kilmaurs)		MacBeth Drive	J7
son Gardens	B8	Haining Avenue	G12	Kilmaurs Road	E4	MacBeth Gardens	J7
Place	C9	Hareshaw Drive	G3	Kilmory Place	E4	MacBeth Walk	J7
Drive	G2	Hareshaw Gardens	G3	King Street	F8	MacCallum Drive	J7
Place	J9	Harperland Drive	D9	Kingsford Place	H3	MacCallum Place	J7
ggan Place	D5	Harriet Road	G6	Kingswell Avenue	G3	MacDonald Drive	J7
ggan Road	D5	Harris Place	H3	Kinloch Road	G11	Macdonald Gardens	J7
yson Drive	K5	Hawthorn Square	D8	Kinnoull Road	G13	MacDonald Place	J7
ace	C9	Hazel Avenue	C9	Kirkton Road	F3	MacDougall Drive (1)	J7
ng Street	E11	Heather Court	E5	Kirktonholm Place	F9	MacDougall Place	J7
Place	F2	Heather Place	D9	Kirktonholm Street	F8	MacEwan Place	J8
s Place	H6	Hestan Place	H3	Kirkwall Place	G3	MacFarlane Drive	J7
s Walk	H6	High Church Lane (1)	F7	Knockando Place	E5	MacGregor Drive	H8
ate, The	F7	High Glencairn Street	F9	Knockinlaw Mount	F4	MacNichol Gardens	J7
ate Square	F7	High Street	G7	Knockinlaw Road	F4	MacNichol Place	J7
t Grove	H3	Highet Street	F6	Knockmarloch Drive	F13	MacInnes Place	J7
Street	E7	Highfield Avenue	G5	Knowehead Road	F12	MacIntosh Place	H7
Place	G11	Highfield Grove	G5	Laburnum Road	C9	MacIntyre Place	J7
s Street	F8	Hill Street	F6	Lagavulin Place	E5	MacIvor Place	J7
r Walk	J6	Hillhead Square	F5	Lainshaw Avenue	E13	MacKellar Place	J6
ton Court (3)	E7	Hillpark Drive	F6	Lamlash Gardens	G4	MacKendrick Place	J8
ton Street	E8	Holehouse Road	G8	Lammermuir Road	G13	*continued overleaf...*

59

KILMARNOCK

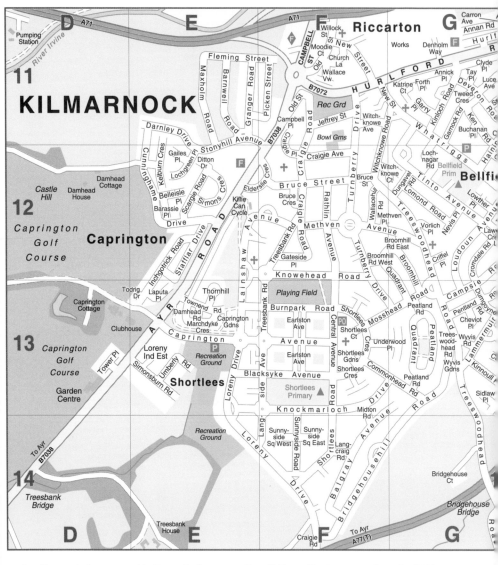

continued from overleaf...		MacPherson Gardens	J7	Meiklewood Road	F4	Moorfield Avenue
		MacPherson Place	J7	Melville Street	H8	Morris Lane
MacKenzie Drive	H7	MacPherson Walk	J7	Merrick Road	H12	Morrison Place
MacKinlay Place	G9	McIlvanney Crescent	F6	Methven Avenue	F12	Morton Place
MacKinnon Drive	J8	McIlvanney Drive	F6	Methven Place	F12	Morven Avenue
MacLaren Place	J8	McLelland Drive	E9	Mews Lane	E9	Mossgiel Avenue
MacLean Drive	H7	Machrie Road	E4	Middlemass Drive	H8	Mosshead Road
MacLeod Drive	J8	Mackie Place	J7	Midton Road	F13	Mosside Place
MacLeod Place	J8	Main Road	K9	Mill Court	G8	Mount Avenue
MacMillan Drive (2)	J7	Manor Avenue	G4	Mill Street	F9	Mount House
MacMillan Place	J7	Manse Street	G8	Millhill Terrace	E3	Mount Place
MacNab Place	H7	Maple Place	D8	Milton Avenue	J7	Mount Pleasant Way
MacNaughton Drive	J7	Marchdyke Crescent	E13	Milton Drive	J7	Mount Village
MacNaughton Walk	J7	Margaret Parker Avenue	D6	Milton Road	J8	Muirend Road
MacNeil Place	H7	Mathew Smith Avenue	E10	Mitchell Court	G8	Muirfield Drive
MacNichol Gardens	J7	Mauchline Court	H2	Montgomery Place	F6	Munro Avenue
MacNichol Place	J7	Maxholm Road	E11	Montgomery Street	F6	Munro Place
MacPhail Drive	H7	Maxwell Court	K5	Moodie Court	F11	Mure Avenue

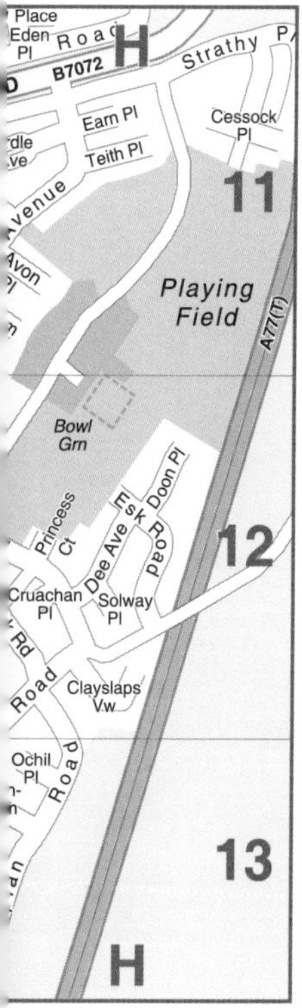

ay Place	J6
on Street	F8
s Place	G12
Mill Road	G9
Street	F11
ands Drive	E4
ands Place	E3
milns Gardens	H2
on Walk	G9
Place	H11
n Court	K4
Gargieston Road	C10
Hamilton Place	E7
Hamilton Street	E8
craig Road	G5
ery Avenue	G8
ery Gardens	G9
ery Lane	H8
ery Street	F9
ery Wynd	G9
Place	D8
Place	H13
tree Place	H2
e Place	J6
vine Road	E8
ill Road	G8
arr Wynd	D5
ome Drive	B9
treet	F10, F11
ant Drive	J8
Road	D8
nk Drive	E4
ard Gardens	G6
ard Street	F6
ey Drive	G3
ey Drive	J9
urn Avenue	H5
Lane	F7

Park Street	E7
Park View	G6
Paxton Place	G9
Peace Avenue	D7
Peatland Quadrant	G13
Peatland Road	G13
Pentland Road	G13
Picken Street	F11
Pine Road	D9
Porter Drive	B10
Porting Cross Place	H2
Portland Place	E8
Portland Road	E8
Portland Street	F7
Portree Avenue	G2
Pottery Place	F6
Priestland Close	H2
Primrose Place	D7
Princes Street	F8
Princess Court	H12
Queen Street	F8
Queen's Drive	G9, H10
Raasay Place	G2
Raithburn Avenue	F4
Ralston Drive	K8
Rankin Court	J5
Rathlin Avenue	F12
Redding Avenue	F4
Rennie Street	G8
Riccarton Road	J10
Richardland Place	G9
Richardland Road (7)	F9
Ritchie Court	J6
Riverbank Place	G9
Robert Creighton Place	F7
Robert Noble Place	D6
Robert Stewart Place (2)	E7
Robertson Place	G8
Rona Place	H3
Rosebank Place	F6
Ross Walk	H6
Rothesay Place	F5
Rousay Wynd	G2
Rowallan Drive	G4, H4
Rowan Place	D9
Rowanhill Place	D9
Rugby Crescent	D9
Rugby Road	D9
Rumford Place	J2
Russell Court	J5
St Andrew's Court (6)	F8
St Andrew's Street	F8
St Andrews Street	F9
St Andrew's Walk	F9
St Marnock Place (5)	F8
St Marnock Street	F8
St Maur's Crescent	E5
St Maur's Place	E5
St Michael's Mount	B9
Samson Avenue	H8
Sanda Place	H2
Sandbed Lane	F8
Sandbed Street	F8
Sannox Road	C6
Scalpay Place	G3
Scargie Road	E12
Scott Crescent	E9
Scott Road	E9, E10
Seaford Street	E8
Seright Crescent	K9
Seright Square	K8
Shanks Court	F6
Shanter Place	J8
Shawbank Place	G9
Shetland Drive	G2
Shiskine Drive	E4
Shortlees Court	F13
Shortlees Crescent	F13
Shortlees Gardens	F13
Shortlees Road	F14
Sidlaw Place	G13

Silverwood Road	K8
Simons Crescent	E12
Simonsburn Road	E13
Simpson Street	A7
Sinclair Court	J5
Skene Road	J5
Skye Gardens	G2
Smiddy Court	F10
Smillie Place	C10
Solway Place	H12
Soulis Street	F7
Souter Drive	J8
South Dean Road	G6
South Gargieston Drive	C10
South Hamilton Court	E8
South Hamilton Place	E9
South Hamilton Street	E9
Southcraig Avenue	J2
Southcraig Drive	G2
Southhook Crescent	D6
Southhook Road	D6
Southhook View	D6
Sparrow Gardens	J9
Spey Avenue	G11
Springhill Gardens	E8
Springhill Place	E8
Springhill Stables	E8
Springhill View	E8
Square of Ales	F7
Stafflar Drive	E12
Stafford Street	F6
Station Drive	K10
Stevenson Court	D7
Stevenson Street	D7
Stewarton Crescent	H2
Stirling Avenue	C7
Stirling Crescent	C7
Stonyhill Avenue	E11
Stornoway Drive	G2
Strand Street	F7
Strawberrybank Road	G6
Stronsay Place	G3
Struthers Avenue	K8
Sturrock Street	F8
Sunnyside Road	F14
Sunnyside Square East	F14
Sunnyside Square West	F14
Sutherland Drive	K5, K7
Swallow Place	J9
Talisker Avenue	D4
Talisker Gardens	E4
Talisker Rigg	D4
Tannock Street	F10
Tarbolton Place	J2
Tay Place	G11
Teith Place	H11
Thirdpart Place	D9
Thomas Baird Gardens	F5
Thomson Street	F6
Thorn Terrace	G4
Thornhill Place	E13
Tinto Avenue	G12
Titchfield Street	F9
Titwood Drive	F4
Tobermory Drive	D5
Todhill Avenue	F4
Todrig Drive	E13
Toponthank Lane	G2
Tourhill Road	E4
Tower Place	D13
Townend Road	E13
Townhead Gardens	G6
Townholm	G6
Treesbank Road	F12, F13
Treeswoodhead Road	G12, G13
Trondra Gardens	G2
Troon Walk	C7
Turnberry Drive	F12
Turner Place	G5

Tweed Crescent	G11
Uist Lane	G2
Umberly Road	E13
Underwood Place	F13
Union Street	F7
Urquhart Road	K6
Vatersay Place	G2
Victoria East Road	G9
Victoria Terrace	G9
Vorlich Place	G12
Vrackie Place	G12
Waddell Court	F4
Walker Avenue	H8
Wallace Street	E9
Wallace View	F11
Wallacehill Road	F12
Wallacetown Avenue	H2
Walnut Road	C9
Wardneuk Drive	F4, G4
Wards Place	F8
Warwickhill Place	E6
Warwickhill Road	D7
Water Lane	F8
Waterside Court	F8
Waterside Street	F8
Watson Street	H8
Waulkmill Place	G9
Waverley Avenue	C7
Welbeck Street	G9
Wellington Avenue	K8
Wellington Place	F6
Wellington Street	F7
Wellpark Avenue	J8
Wellpark Court	J8
Wellpark Grove	J8
Wellpark Place	J8
West Fullarton Street	E7
West George Street	F7
West Langlands Street	E7
West Netherton Street	F9
West Shaw Street	F9
West Woodstock Court	E8
West Woodstock Street	E8
Western Place	G4
Western Road	D6, F5, G4
Westfield Road	J2
Westmoor Crescent	D9
Westray Drive	G2
Whatriggs Road	G11
William Street	F6
Willie Mairs Brae	G6
Willie Ross Place	K4
Willock Street	F11
Willow Road	D8
Wilson Avenue	G8
Witch Road	F6
Witchill Place	F6
Witchknowe Avenue	F11
Witchknowe Court	F12
Witchknowe Road	F12
Woodhill Road	E5
Woodlands Grove	H4
Woodlands Place	H4
Woodside Avenue	D10
Woodstock Place	E7
Woodstock Street	E8
Wyvis Gardens	G13
Wyvis Road	G13
Yorke Place	D7

KILWINNING

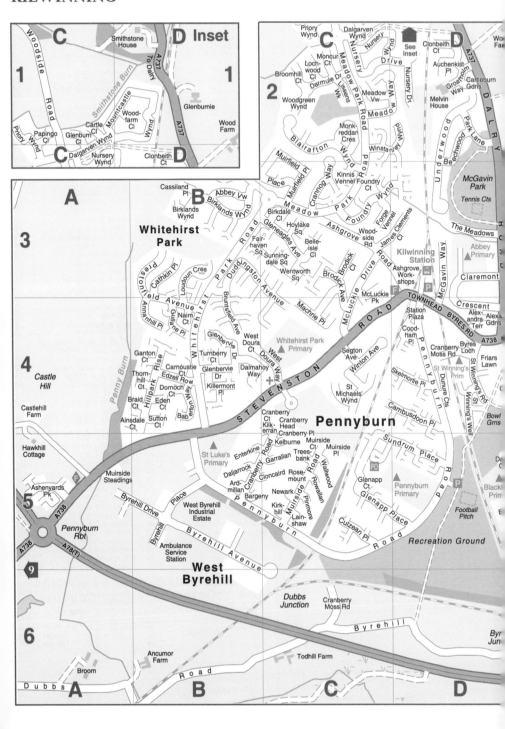

Inset

C D

1 1

Smithstone House
Woodside Road
To Dalry
A737
Smithstone Burn
Mountcastle Wynd
Glenburnie
Wood-farm Cl
Carlie Cl
Wood Farm
Priory Wynd
Papingo Cl
Glenburn Cl
Dalgarven Wynd
Nursery Wynd
Clonbeith Ct

Priory Wynd — **Dalgarven Wynd** — Nursery
See Inset
Clonbeith Ct
Moncur Ct
Loch-wood Cl
Meadow Park Road
Drive
Nursery Dr
Auchenkist Pl
Broomhill Ct
Darmule Dr
Lissens Wk
Groatholm Way
Cartleburn Gdns
Woodgreen Wynd
Meadow Vw
Meadow Vw
Melvin House
Meadow
DALRY
Monk-reddan Cres
Winstanley
Park Lane
Blairafton
Muirfield Pl
Muirfield Pl
Cranmog Way
Kinnis Vennel
Foundry Ct
Underwood
Beechwood
McGavin Park
Place
Meadow Park
Foundry Wynd
Tennis Cts
Cassiland Pl
Abbey Vw
Birklands Wynd
Birkdale Cl
Ashgrove Road
Forge Vennel
James Clements Cl
The Meadows
Birklands Wynd
Hoylake Sq
Wood-side Rd
Abbey Primary
Whitehirst Park
Gleneagles Ave
Belle-isle Cl
Brodick Ave
Kilwinning Station
Ashgrove Work-shops
Claremont
Fair-haven Sq
Sunning-dale Sq
Wentworth Sq
Brodick Cl
McLuckie Cl
McGavin Way
Pressfield Avenue
Cathkin Pl
Loudoun Cres
Dudingston Avenue
Machrie Pl
McLuckie Pk
McLuckie Drive
Crescent
Alexandra Terr
Alexa Gdns
Annanhill Pl
Nairn Ct
Guilane Pl
Brunsfield Ave
West Doura Ct
West Doura Way
Station Plaza
Coodham Pl
Byres Loch
Byres Rd
Friars Lawn
Glenbervie Dr
TOWNHEAD
BYRES RD
A738
Ganton Ct
Turnberry Ct
Whitehirst Park Primary
Segton Ave
Winton Ave
Cranberry Moss Rd
St Winning's Prim
Thorn-hill Ct
Carnoustie Ct
Edzell Row
Glenbervie Dr
Dalmahoy Way
Skelmorlie Pl
Dunure Cts
St Winning's Rd
Braid Ct
Dornoch Ct
Killermont Pl
St Michaels' Wynd
Cambusdoon Pl
Bowl Grns
Ainsdale Ct
Sutton Ct
Eden Ct
Bab
Castle Hill
Hillpark Rise
Penny Burn
STEVENSTON
Cranberry Ct
Kilk-erran
Cranberry Head
Cranberry Pl
Pennyburn
Sundrum Place
Castlehill Farm
Kelburne
Muirside Ct
Muirside Pl
Hawkhill Cottage
St Luke's Primary
Enterkine
Treesbank
Glenapp Ct
Pennyburn Primary
Blackland Prim
Muirside Steadings
Daljarrock
Garrallan
Cranberry Road
Cloncaird
Rose-mount
Rowallan
Wallwood
Football Pitch
Ashenyards Pk
Byrehill Drive
Place
Ard-millan
Bargeny
Newark Pl
Pirnmore
Glenapp Place
Recreation Ground
A738
Pennyburn Rbt
Kirk-hill
Lain-shaw
Culzean Pl
Byrehill
Road
A78(T)
West Byrehill Industrial Estate
Byrehill Avenue
Pennyburn
A738
Ambulance Service Station
West Byrehill
Dubbs Junction
Cranberry Moss Rd
Byrehill
Byr Jun
Ancumor Farm
Todhill Farm
Broom
Road
Dubbs

A B C D

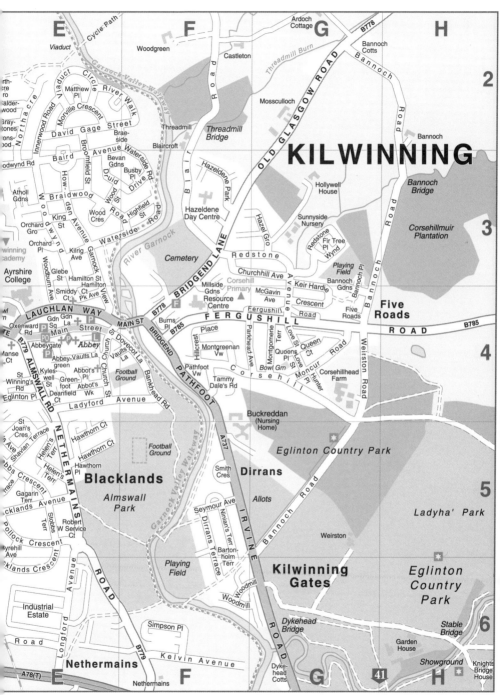

KILWINNING

Index to street names can be found starting on page 101

KIRKOSWALD & LARGS

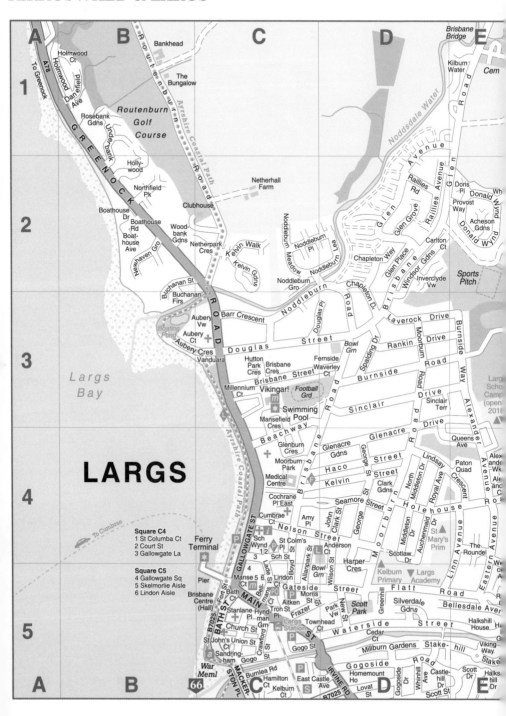

Square C4
1 St Columba Ct
2 Court St
3 Gallowgate La

Square C5
4 Gallowgate Sq
5 Skelmorlie Aisle
6 Lindon Aisle

LARGS

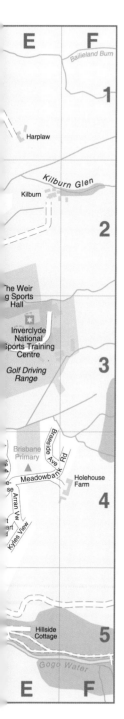

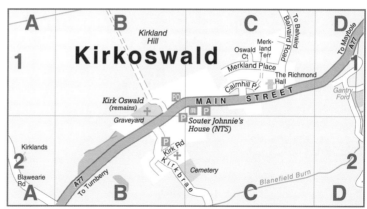

Kirkoswald

Index to Kirkoswald

Balvaird Road	C1
Blawearie Road	A2
Cairnhill Place	C1
Kirk Road	B2
Kirkbrae	B2
Oswald Court	C1
Main Street	C1
Merkland Place	C1
Merkland Terrace	C1

Index to Largs

Acheson Gardens	E2	Bowen Craig	D7	Fernside	D3
Acre Avenue	D7	Bowen Craig Walk	D8	Flatt Road	D5
Aitken Street	C5	Boyd Street	C4	Fort Street	C5
Alexander Avenue	E3	Braeside Avenue	E4	Frazer Street	C5
Alexander Court	E4	Brisbane Crescent	C3	Gallowgate Lane (3)	C4
Alexander Walk	E4	Brisbane Glen Road	D3	Gallowgate Square (4)	C4
Allanpark Street	C4	Brisbane Road	C4	Gallowgate Street	C5
Amy Place	C4	Brisbane Street	C3	Gateside Street	C5
Anderson Court	D4	Broom Court	D6	George Street	D4
Anthony Court	D7	Broomfield	C6	Glen Avenue	D2
Anthony Road	D7	Broomfield Crescent	C6	Glen Grove	D2
Arran View	E4	Broomfield Place	C6	Glen Place	D2
Aubrey Court	B3	Broomknowe	D7	Glenacre Drive	D4
Aubrey Crescent	B3	Broompark	D7	Glenacre Gardens	D4
Aubrey View	C3	Buchanan Firs	B3	Glenburn Crescent	C4
Auchenmaid Drive	D4	Buchanan Street	B2	Gogo Street	C5
Bankhouse Avenue	D6	Burnlea Road	C5	Gogoside Drive	D5
Bankhouse Crescent	D6	Burnside Road	D3	Gogoside Road	D5
Bankhouse Grove	E6	Burnside Way	E3	Greenhill	D5
Barr Crescent	C3	Carlton Court	D2	Greenock Road	B1
Bath Court	C5	Castle Bay Court	C6	Greeto Falls Avenue	E4
Bath Street	C5	Castlehill Drive	D5	Haco Street	D4
Beachway	C4	Cathcart Road	D6	Halkshill Drive	E5
Bellesdale Avenue	E5	Cedar Court	D5	Halkshill Gardens	E5
Bellmans Close	C5	Chapelton Drive	D2	Halkshill House	E5
Blackdales Avenue	D6	Chapelton Way	D2	Hamilton Court	C5
Blythswood Crescent	D6	Charles Street	C6	Hamilton Drive	D6
Boathouse Avenue	B2	Church Street	C5	Harper Crescent	D4
Boathouse Drive	B2	Clark Gardens	D4	Haylie Brae	E7
Boathouse Road	B2	Cochrane Place East	C4	Haylie Gardens	D6
		Court Street (2)	C4	Haylie Neuk	D6
		Crawford Street	C5	Hill Street	C6
		Cumbrae Court	C4	Holehouse Court	E4
		Cunningham Drive	D6	Holehouse Road	D4
		Curlinghall	D6	Hollywood	B2
		Dalry Road	E7	Holmwood	A1
		Danefield Avenue	B1	Holmwood Court	B1
		Donald Wynd	E2	Homemount House	D5
		Doris Place	E2	Hutcheson Drive	D7
		Douglas Place	C3	Hutton Park Crescent	C3
		Douglas Street	C3	Hyndman Green	C5
		Duffield Drive	D7	Inverclyde View	D2
		East Castle Avenue	C5	Irvine Road	D5, E8
		Eastern Avenue	E5	John Clark Street	D4
		Eldslie Gardens	C6	continued overleaf...

LARGS, LOGAN & LUGAR

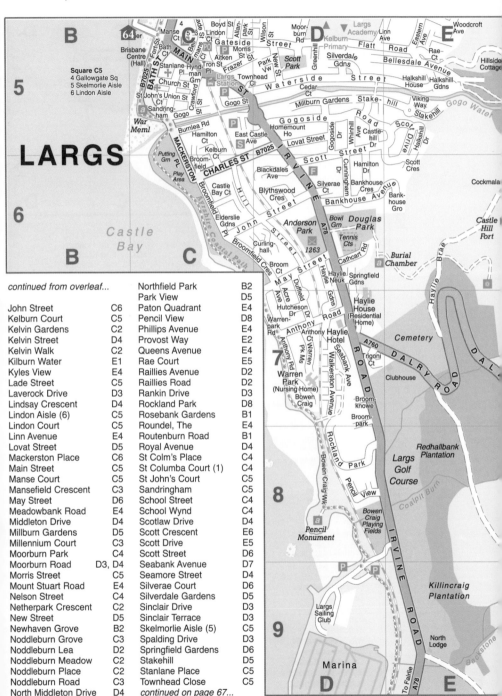

Square C5
4 Gallowgate Sq
5 Skelmorlie Aisle
6 Lindon Aisle

continued from overleaf...

John Street	C6	Northfield Park	B2
Kelburn Court	C5	Park View	D5
Kelvin Gardens	C2	Paton Quadrant	E4
Kelvin Street	D4	Pencil View	D8
Kelvin Walk	C2	Phillips Avenue	E4
Kilburn Water	E1	Provost Way	E2
Kyles View	E4	Queens Avenue	E4
Lade Street	C5	Rae Court	E5
Laverock Drive	D3	Raillies Avenue	D2
Lindsay Crescent	D4	Raillies Road	D2
Lindon Aisle (6)	C5	Rankin Drive	D3
Lindon Court	C5	Rockland Park	D8
Linn Avenue	E4	Rosebank Gardens	B1
Lovat Street	D5	Roundel, The	E4
Mackerston Place	C6	Routenburn Road	B1
Main Street	C5	Royal Avenue	D4
Manse Court	C5	St Colm's Place	C4
Mansefield Crescent	C3	St Columba Court (1)	C4
May Street	D6	St John's Court	C5
Meadowbank Road	E4	Sandringham	C5
Middleton Drive	D4	School Street	C4
Millburn Gardens	D5	School Wynd	C4
Millennium Court	C3	Scotlaw Drive	D4
Moorburn Park	C4	Scott Crescent	E6
Moorburn Road	D3, D4	Scott Drive	E5
Morris Street	C5	Scott Street	D6
Mount Stuart Road	E4	Seabank Avenue	D7
Nelson Street	C4	Seamore Street	D4
Netherpark Crescent	C2	Silverae Court	D6
New Street	D5	Silverdale Gardens	D5
Newhaven Grove	B2	Sinclair Drive	D3
Noddleburn Grove	C3	Sinclair Terrace	D3
Noddleburn Lea	D2	Skelmorlie Aisle (5)	C5
Noddleburn Meadow	C2	Spalding Drive	D3
Noddleburn Place	C2	Springfield Gardens	D6
Noddleburn Road	C3	Stakehill	D5
North Middleton Drive	D4	Stanlane Place	C5
		Townhead Close	C5

continued on page 67...

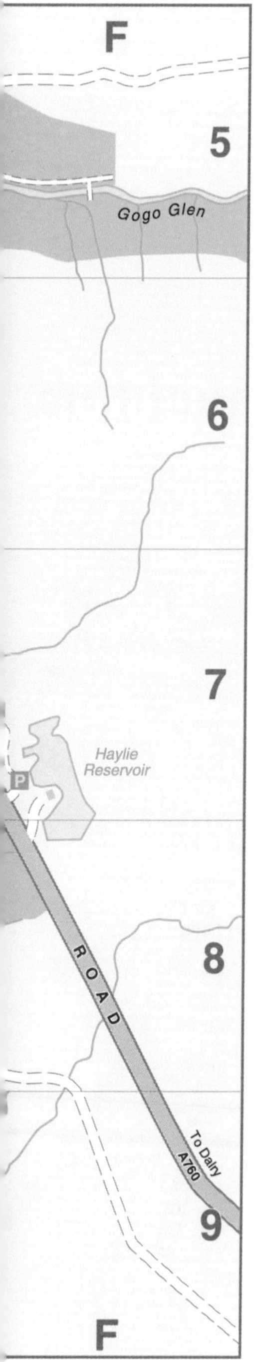
F
5
Gogo Glen
6
7
Haylie Reservoir
P
8
ROAD
To Dalry
A760
9
F

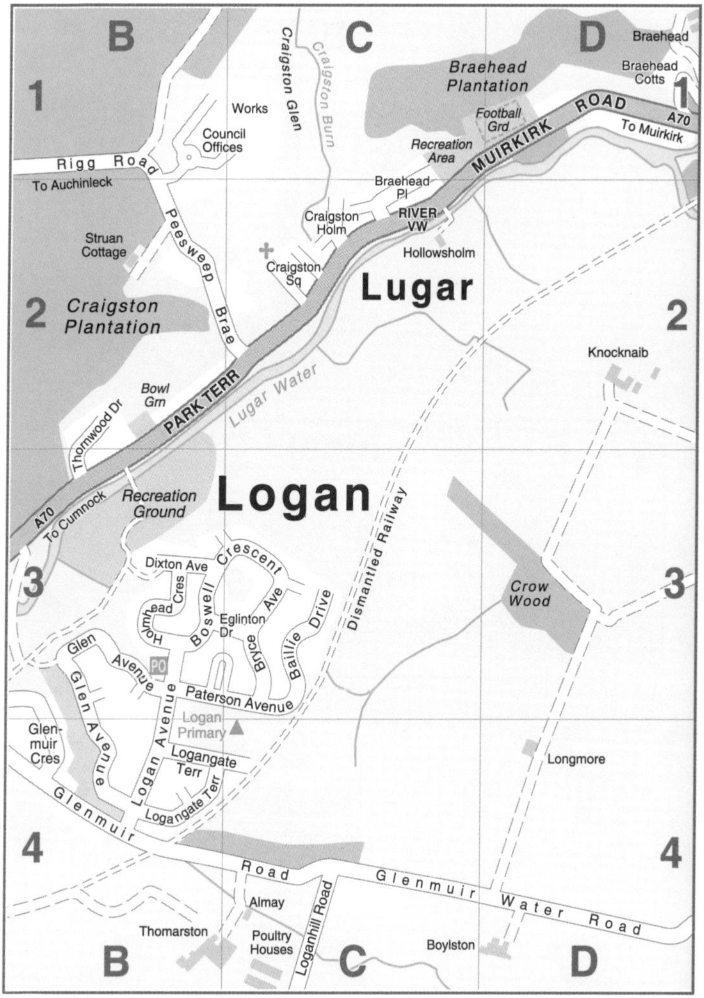
B
C
D
Braehead
Craigston Glen
Craigston Burn
Braehead Plantation
Braehead Cotts
1
Works
Council Offices
Football Grd
ROAD
A70
MUIRKIRK
To Muirkirk
Rigg Road
To Auchinleck
Recreation Area
Braehead Pl
Peesweep Brae
Craigston Holm
RIVER VW
Struan Cottage
Hollowsholm
Craigston Sq
Lugar
2
Craigston Plantation
2
Knocknaib
Bowl Grn
Lugar Water
PARK TERR
Thornwood Dr
Logan
Recreation Ground
A70
To Cumnock
Dismantled Railway
Dixton Ave
Crescent
Cres
3
Holmhead
Boswell
Eglinton Dr
Ave
Crow Wood
3
Baillie Drive
Bryce
Glen
Avenue
PO
Paterson Avenue
Glen Avenue
Logan Avenue
Logan Primary
Glen-muir Cres
Logangate Terr
Longmore
Logangate Terr
Glenmuir
4
4
Road
Glenmuir Water Road
Almay
Thomarston
Loganhill Road
Poultry Houses
Boylston
B
C
D

continued from page 66...

Trigoni Court D7
Tron Place C5
Underbank B1
Union Street C5
Vanduara C3
Viking Way E5
Walkerston Avenue D7
Warren Park Mews D7
Warrenpark Road D7
Waterside Street D5
Waverley Court D3
Whinhill Avenue D5
White Court E2
Wilson Street D5
Windsor Gardens D2
Woodbank Gardens B2
Woodcroft Avenue E5

Index to Logan & Lugar

Baillie Drive C3
Boswell Crescent B3
Braehead Cottages D1
Braehead Place C2
Bryce Avenue C3
Craigston Holm C2
Craigston Square C2
Dixton Avenue B3
Eglinton Drive C3
Glen Avenue B3
Glenmuir Crescent B4
Glenmuir Road B4
Glenmuir Water Road C4
Holmhead Crescent B3
Logan Avenue B4
Logangate Terrace B4
Loganhill Road C4
Muirkirk Road C1
Park Terrace B2
Paterson Avenue B3
Peesweep Brae B2
Rigg Road B1
River View C2
Thornwood Drive B2

MAUCHLINE & MAIDENS

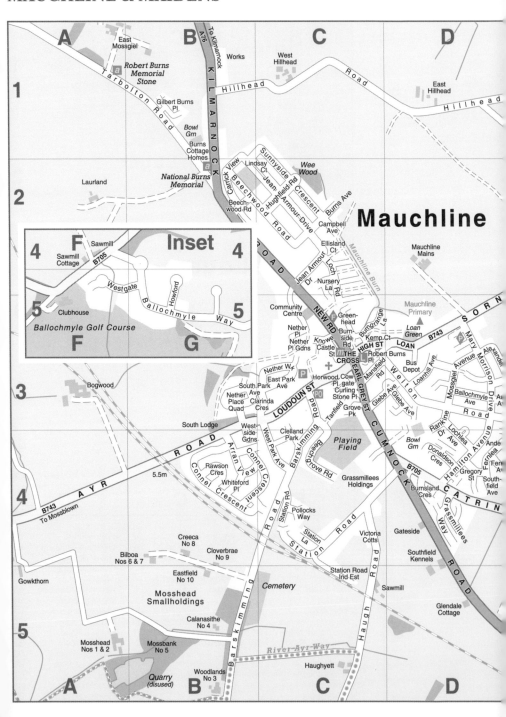

Mauchline

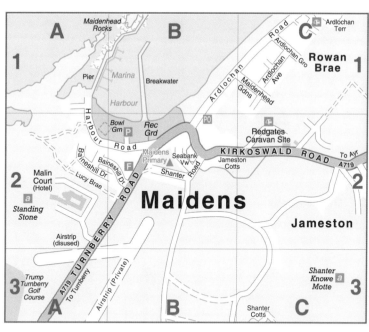

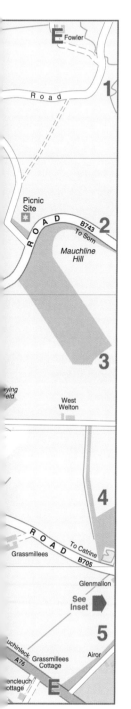

Index to Mauchline

		Gilbert Burns	B1	Rankine Drive	D3	
		Place		Rawson Crescent	B4	
Alexander Terrace	D3	Glebe Avenue	C3, D3	Robert Burns Place	C3	
Anderson Avenue	D4	Grassmillees Way	D4	Sorn Road	D3	
Arran View	B4	Greenhead	C3	South Park Avenue	B3	
Auld Avenue	D3	Gregory Street	D4	Southfield Avenue	D4	
Ayr Road	A4	Grove Park	C3	Station Lane	C4	
Ballochmyle Avenue	D3	Hamilton Avenue	D4	Station Road	C4	
Ballochmyle Way	G5	Haugh Road	C5	Sunnyside Crescent	C2	
Barskimming Road	B5, C4	High Street	C3	Tanfield	C3	
Beechgrove Road	C4	Hillhead Road	B1, D1	Tarbolton Road	A1	
Beechwood Road	B2	Horwood Place	C3	Victoria Cottages	C4	
Burngrange Lane	C3	Howford	G5	Waterside Gardens	B4	
Burns Avenue	C2	Hughfield Road	C2	Welton Road	D3	
Burns Cottage	B1	Jean Armour Drive	C2	West Park Avenue	C4	
Homes		Kemp Court	C3	Westgate	F5	
Burnside Road	C3	Kilmarnock Road	B1	Whiteford Place	B4	
Burnsland Crescent	D4	Knowe	C3			
Campbell Avenue	C2	Lindsay Court	C2	**Index to Maidens**		
Carrick View	B2	Loan	D3			
Castle Street	C3	Loanhill Avenue	D3	Ardlochan Avenue	C1	
Catrine Road	D4	Loch Road	C2	Ardlochan Grove	C1	
Clarinda Crescent	C3	Lochlea Avenue	D3	Ardlochan Road	B1	
Clelland Park	C4	Loudoun Street	C3	Ardlochan Terrace	C1	
Connel Crescent	B4	Mansfield Road	C3	Baineshill Drive	A2	
Cowgate	C3	Mary Morrison Drive	D3	Harbour Road	A1	
Cross, The	C3	Mossgiel Avenue	D3	Jameston Cottages	B2	
Cumnock Road	C3	Nether Place	C3	Kirkoswald Road	C2	
Curling Stone Place	C3	Nether Place Gardens	C3	Lucy Brae	A2	
Donaldson Crescent	D4	Nether Place Quadrant	B3	Maidenhead Gardens	C1	
Earl Grey Street	C3	Nether Walk	C3	Seabank View	B2	
East Park Avenue	C4	New Road	C3	Shanter Cottages	C3	
Ellisland Court	C2	Nursery Lane	C2	Shanter Road	B2	
Fernlea Avenue	D4	Pollocks Way	C4	Turnberry Road	A3	

MAYBOLE & MINISHANT

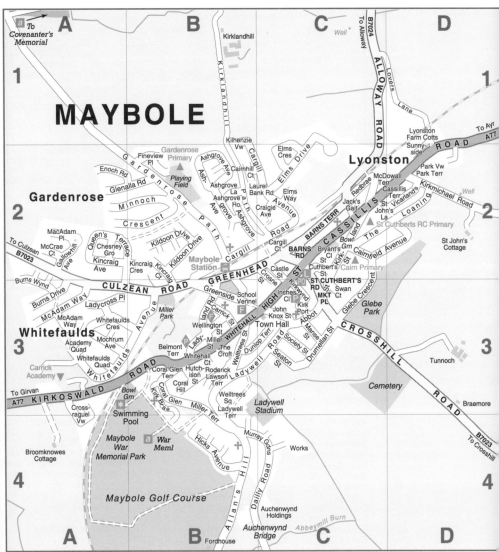

Index to Maybole

		Belmont Terrace	B3	Castle Street	C
		Bryant's Close	C2	Chesney Grove	A
Abbot Street	C3	Burns Drive	A3	Coral Glen	B
Academy Quadrant	A3	Burns Wynd	A3	Coral Glen Terrace	B
Allan's Hill	B4	Cairnfield Avenue	C2	Coral Hill	B
Alloway Road	C1	Cairnhill Court	B2	Craigie Avenue	C
Ashgrove	B2	Cargill Avenue	C2	Croft, The	B
Ashgrove Avenue	B2	Cargill Court	C2	Crosne Street	C
Ashgrove House	B2	Cargill Road	B2	Crosshill Road	C
Ashgrove Lane	B2	Carrick Street	B3	Crossraguel View	A
Barns Road	C2	Cassillis Road	C2	Culzean Road	B
Barns Terrace	C2	Cassillis Terrace	D2	Dailly Road	C

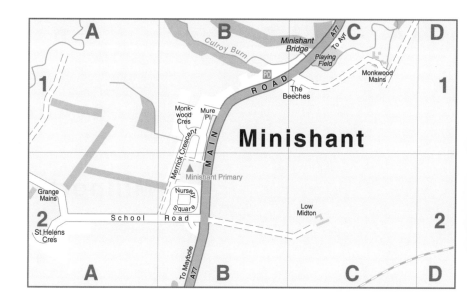

Drumellan Street	C3	Lovers Lane	D1
Dunlop Terrace	B3	Lyonston Farm	D1
Elms Crescent	C2	Cottages	
Elms Drive	C2	MacAdam Place	A2
Elms Way	C2	McAdam Way	A3
Enoch Road	A2	McCrae Court	A2
Fineview Place	B2	McDowall Terrace	C2
Gallowhill Avenue	A2	Manse Street	C3
Gardenrose Path	B2	Market Place	C3
Glebe Crescent	C3	Miller Street	B3
Glenalla Road	A2	Miller Terrace	B3
Greenhead	B3	Minnoch Crescent	A2
Greenside	B3	Mochrum Avenue	A3
Hicks Avenue	B4	Murray Gardens	B4
High Street	C3	Park Terrace	D2
Hutchison Street	B3	Park View	D2
Inches Close	C3	Queen's Terrace	A2
Jack's Gait	C2	Redbrae	C2
John Knox Street	C3	Roderick Lawson	B3
Kildoon Drive	B2	Terrace	
Kilhenzie View	B1	St Cuthberts Road	C3
Kincraig Avenue	A2	St Cuthberts Street	C2
Kincraig Court	B2	St John's Lane	D2
Kincraig Crescent	B2	School Vennel	B3
Kirk Brae	B3	Seaton Street	C3
Kirkland Street	C2	Society Street	C3
Kirklandhill Path	B1	Sunnyside	D2
Kirkmichael Road	D2	Swan Court	C3
Kirkoswald Road	A3	Vicarlands	D2
Kirk Port	C3	Wellington Street	B3
Kirk Wynd	C3	Welltrees Square	B3
Ladycross Place	A3	Welltrees Street	B3
Ladyland Road	B3	Whitefaulds Avenue	A3
Ladywell Road	B3	Whitefaulds Crescent	A3
Ladywell Terrace	B3	Whitefaulds Quadrant	A3
Laurel Bank Road	B2	Whitehall	B3
Loaning, The	D2	Whitehall Court	B3

Index to Minishant

Beeches, The	C1
Merrick Crescent	B2
Monkwood Crescent	B1
Mure Place	B1
Nursery Square	B2
St Helens Crescent	A2
School Road	A2

MILLPORT

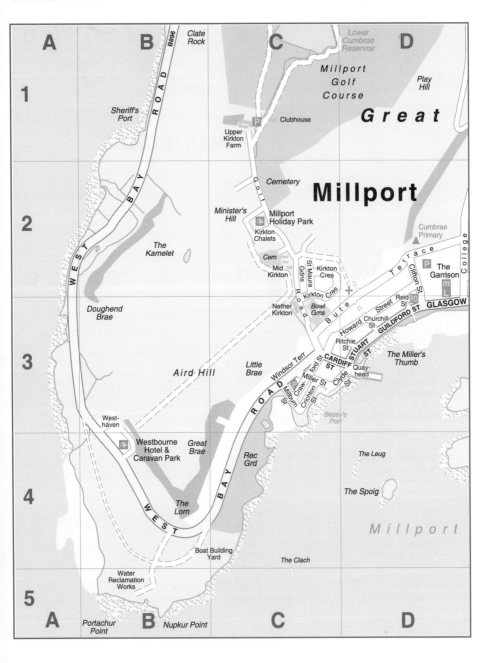

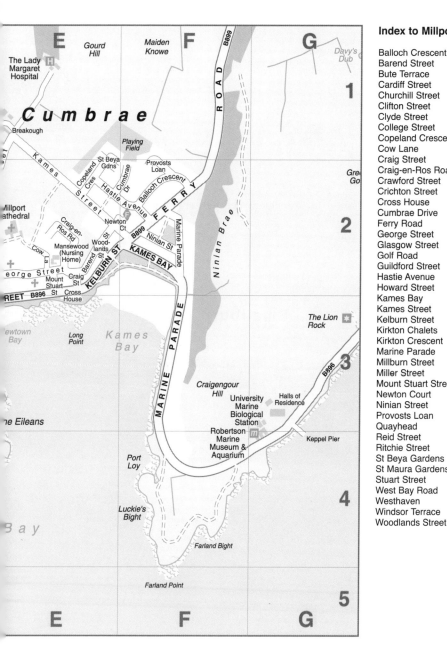

Index to Millport

Balloch Crescent	F2
Barend Street	E2
Bute Terrace	C3
Cardiff Street	C3
Churchill Street	D3
Clifton Street	D2
Clyde Street	D3
College Street	D2
Copeland Crescent	E2
Cow Lane	E2
Craig Street	E2
Craig-en-Ros Road	E2
Crawford Street	C3
Crichton Street	C3
Cross House	E3
Cumbrae Drive	F2
Ferry Road	F2
George Street	E2
Glasgow Street	D3
Golf Road	C2
Guildford Street	D3
Hastie Avenue	E2
Howard Street	D3
Kames Bay	F2
Kames Street	E1
Kelburn Street	E2
Kirkton Chalets	C2
Kirkton Crescent	C2
Marine Parade	F2, F3
Millburn Street	C3
Miller Street	C3
Mount Stuart Street	E2
Newton Court	F2
Ninian Street	F2
Provosts Loan	F2
Quayhead	D3
Reid Street	D3
Ritchie Street	D3
St Beya Gardens	E2
St Maura Gardens	C2
Stuart Street	D3
West Bay Road	A2, B4
Westhaven	B3
Windsor Terrace	C3
Woodlands Street	E2

MUIRKIRK

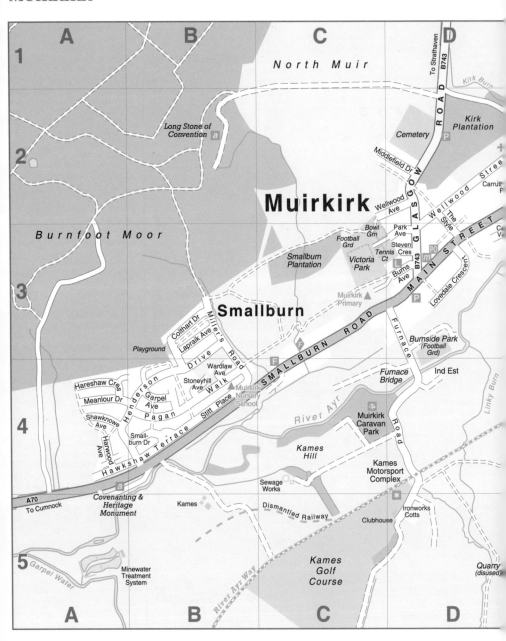

North Muir

Long Stone of Convention

Cemetery

Kirk Plantation

To Strathaven

B743

Kitk Burn

Middlefield Dr

GLASGOW ROAD

Carruth

Muirkirk

Wellwood Ave

Wellwood Street

The Style

Burnfoot Moor

Bowl Grn

Park Ave

Football Grd

Steven Cres

Smallburn Plantation

Tennis Ct

Victoria Park

Burns Ave

MAIN STREET

B743

Lovedale Crescent

Muirkirk Primary

Smallburn

Colthart Dr

Lapraik Ave

Miller's Road

SMALLBURN ROAD

Furnace

Burnside Park (Football Grd)

Playground

Drive

Wardlaw Ave

Stoneyhill Ave

Walk

F

Furnace Bridge

Ind Est

Linky Burn

Hareshaw Cres

Henderson

Garpel Ave

Pagan

Muirkirk Nursery School

Stitt Place

Meanlour Dr

Shawknowe Ave

Harwood Ave

Smallburn Dr

Hawkshaw Terrace

River Ayr

Muirkirk Caravan Park

Road

Kames Hill

Kames Motorsport Complex

A70 To Cumnock

Covenanting & Heritage Monument

Kames

Sewage Works

Dismantled Railway

Ironworks Cotts

Clubhouse

Garpel Water

Minewater Treatment System

River Ayr Way

Kames Golf Course

Quarry (disused)

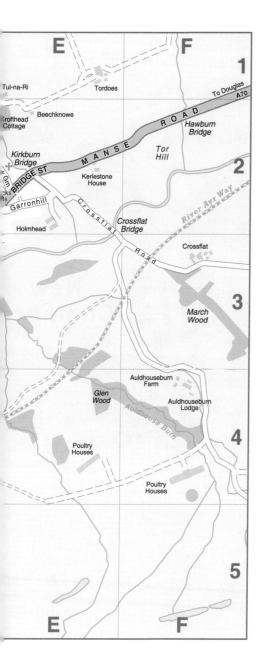

Index to Muirkirk

Bridge Street	E2
Burns Avenue	D3
Cairn View	D3
Carruthers Park	D2
Colthart Drive	B3
Crossflat Road	E2
Furnace Road	D3
Garpel Avenue	B4
Garronhill	E2
Glasgow Road	D3
Hareshaw Crescent	A4
Harwood Avenue	A4
Hawkshaw Terrace	A4
Henderson Drive	A4
Ironworks Cottages	D5
Jacks Mews	E2
Kirk Green	E2
Lapraik Avenue	B3
Lovedale Crescent	D3
Main Street	D3
Manse Road	E2
Meanlour Drive	A4
Middlefield Drive	D2
Miller's Road	B3
Pagan Walk	B4
Park Avenue	D3
Shawknowe Avenue	A4
Smallburn Drive	B4
Smallburn Road	C4
Steven Crescent	D3
Stitt Place	B4
Stoneyhill Avenue	B4
Style, The	D3
Wardlaw Avenue	B4
Wellwood Avenue	D2
Wellwood Street	D2

NEW CUMNOCK

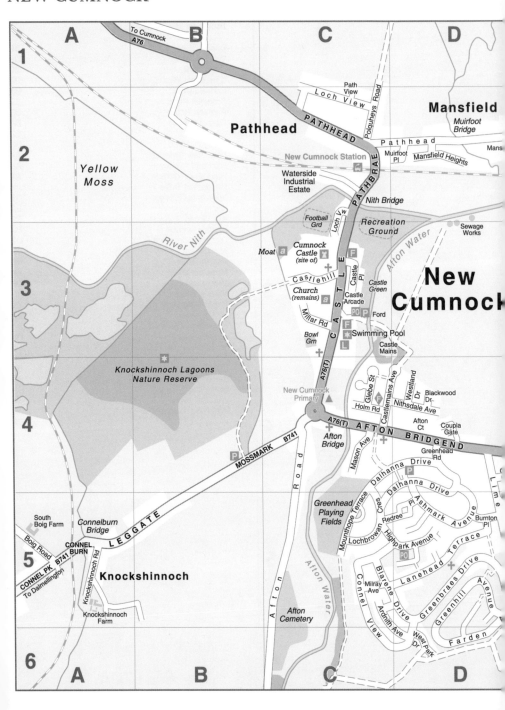

To Cumnock A76

Mansfield

Muirfoot Bridge

Pathhead

Muirfoot Pl

Mansfield Heights

Mans

Path View

Loch View

Polquheys Road

PATHHEAD

Pathhead

PATHBRAE

New Cumnock Station

Waterside Industrial Estate

Nith Bridge

Yellow Moss

River Nith

Football Grd

Loch Vw

Recreation Ground

Afton Water

Sewage Works

Moat

Cumnock Castle
(site of)

Castlehill

Castle Pl

F

Castle Green

New Cumnock

Church
(remains)

Castle Arcade

Castle Mains

PO P Ford

Millar Rd

Bowl Grn

CASTLE

A76(T)

F

Swimming Pool

L

Castle Mains

Knockshinnoch Lagoons Nature Reserve

New Cumnock Primary

Glebe St

Dr

Westland

Blackwood

Holm Rd

Nithsdale Ave

Castlemains Ave

Afton Ct

Coupla Gate

A76(T) AFTON BRIDGEND

MOSSMARK

B741

Road

Afton Bridge

Mason Ave

Greenhead Rd

Lime

Greenhead Playing Fields

Mounthope Terrace

Dalhanna Drive

Dalhanna Drive

Ashmark Avenue

Burnton Pl

South Boig Farm

Connelburn Bridge

LEGGATE

Knockshinnoch Rd

CONNEL BURN

Redree

Lochbrowan Cres

Highpark Avenue

PO

Boig Road

CONNEL PK B741 Rd

To Dalmellington

Knockshinnoch

Knockshinnoch Farm

Afton

Afton Water

Afton Cemetery

Milray Ave

Blayene Drive

Ardnith Ave

Connel View

Lanehead Terrace

Greenbraes Drive

Greenhill Avenue

West Park Dr

Farden

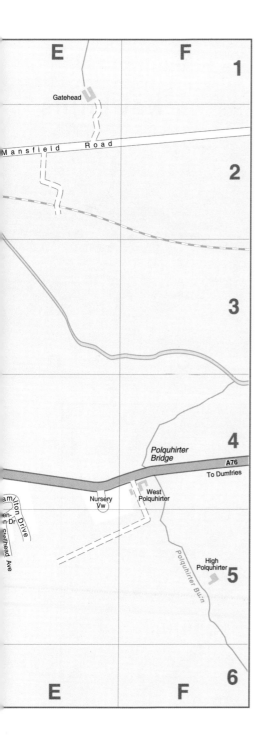

Index to New Cumnock

Afton Bridgend	C4
Afton Court	D4
Afton Road	C5
Ardnith Avenue	C5
Ashmark Avenue	D5
Blackwood Drive	D4
Blarene Drive	C5
Boig Road	A5
Burnton Place	D5
Cairnhill Place	D4
Castle Arcade	C3
Castle Place	C3
Castlehill	C3
Castlemains Avenue	C4
Connel Burn	A5
Connel Park	A5
Connell View	C5
Coupla Gate	D4
Dalhanna Drive	D4
Farden Avenue	D6
Glebe Street	C4
Glenafton Drive	E5
Greenbraes Drive	D5
Greenhead Road	D4
Greenhill Avenue	D5
Hamilton Drive	D5, E4
Highpark Avenue	D5
Holm Road	C4
Knockshinnoch Road	A5
Lanehead Terrace	D5
Leggate	A5
Lime Road	D4
Loch View (New Cumnock)	C3
Loch View (Pathhead)	C2
Lochbrowan Crescent	C5
Mansfield Court	D2
Mansfield Heights	D2
Mansfield Road	E2
Mason Avenue	C4
Millar Road	C3
Milray Avenue	C5
Mossmark	B4
Mounthope Terrace	C5
Muirfoot Place	D2
Nithsdale Avenue	D4
Nursery View	E4
Pathbrae	C2
Pathhead	C2
Path View	C2
Polquheys Road	C2
Redree Place	D5
Stellhead Avenue	E6
West Park Drive	D6
Westland Drive	D4

NEWMILNS, OCHILTREE & SORN

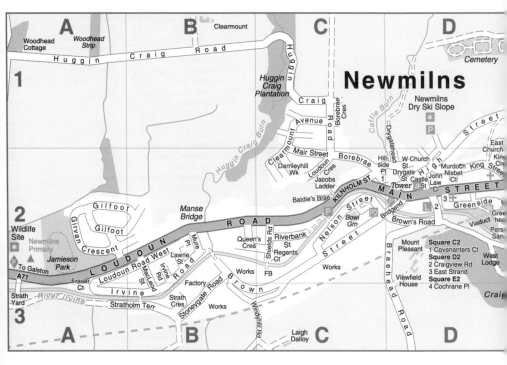

Newmilns

Woodhead Cottage
Woodhead Strip
Clearmount
Huggin Craig Road
Huggin Craig Plantation
Cemetery
Huggin Craig Burn
Craig Avenue
Craig Road
Borebrae Cres
Cattle Burn
Newmilns Dry Ski Slope
East Church
Clearmount
Mair Street
Damleyhill Wk
Loudoun Cres
Jacobs Ladder
Borebrae
Hillside Pl
W Church St
Drygate St
Murdoch St
John Law Ct
Nisbet Ct
King St
King Street
Kin Cre
Baldie's Brae
KILNHOLM ST
Tower
Castle St
MAIN STREET
Drygatehead
Drygate Burn
High Street
Gilfoot
Manse Bridge
Nelson Street
Bowl Grn
Bridgend
Brown's Road
Greenside
Gre hea
Pers San
Viaduct
Wildlife Site
Newmilns Primary
Jamieson Park
Gilfoot
Girvan Crescent
LOUDOUN ROAD
Queen's Cres
Shields Rd
Riverbank St
Regents Ct
Mount Pleasant
Braehead Road
West Lodge
To Galston
A71
Loudoun Road West
Lawrie St
Irvine Rd
Mure Pl
MacLeod St
FB
Works
Works
Viewfield House
Strath Yard
River Irvine
Fraser Ct
Irvine
Strath Cres
Factory
Stoneygate Road
Brown
Works
Stratholm Terr
Laigh Dalloy
Craig

Square C2
1 Covenanters Ct
Square D2
2 Craigview Rd
3 East Strand
Square E2
4 Cochrane Pl

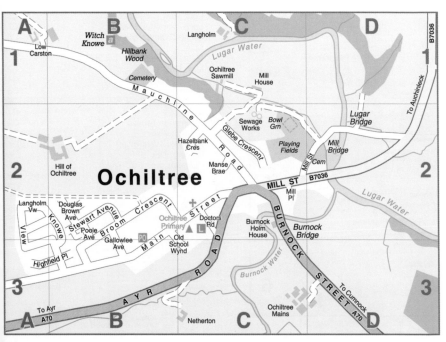

Ochiltree

Low Carston
Witch Knowe
Hillbank Wood
Langholm
Lugar Water
B7036
Cemetery
Mauchline
Ochiltree Sawmill
Mill House
To Auchinleck
Lugar Bridge
Hill of Ochiltree
Hazelbank Cres
Sewage Works
Bowl Grn
Glebe Crescent
Road
Playing Fields
Mill St
Mill Bridge
Cem
Langholm Vw
Douglas Brown Ave
Manse Brae
MILL ST
B7036
Mill Pl
Lugar Water
Knowe
Stewart Avenue
Broom Crescent
Ochiltree Primary
Doctors Rd
Burnock Holm House
Burnock Bridge
View
Poole Ave
Gallowlee Ave
Main Street
Old School Wynd
BURNOCK
Burnock Bridge
Highfield Pl
AYR ROAD
Burnock Water
STREET A70
To Ayr
A70
Netherton
Ochiltree Mains
To Cumnock

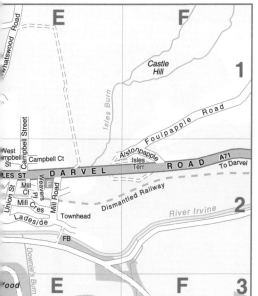

East Strand (3)	D2	Townhead	E2
Foulpapple Road	F2	Union Street	E2
Fraser Court	A3	Weavers Place	E2
Gilfoot	A2	West Campbell Street	E2
Girvan Crescent	A2	West Church Street	D2
Greenhead	D2	Windyhill Road	C3
Greenside	D2		
High Street	D2		
Hillside Place	C2		

Index to Ochiltree

Huggin Craig Road	A1, C1	Ayr Road	B3
Irvine Road	A3	Broom Crescent	B2
Isles Street	E2	Burnock Street	C2
Isles Terrace	F2	Doctor's Road	C2
Jacobs Ladder	C2	Douglas Brown	B2
John Law Close	D2	Avenue	
Kilnholm Street	C2	Gallowlee Avenue	B3
Kings Crescent	D2	Glebe Crescent	C2
King Street	D2	Hazelbank Crescent	C2
Ladeside	E2	Highfield Place	A3
Lawrie Street	B2	Knowe View	B2
Loudoun Crescent	C2	Langholm View	A2
Loudoun Road	A2	Main Street	B3
Loudoun Road West	A2	Manse Brae	C2
MacLeod Street	B2	Mauchline Road	B1
Main Street	C2	Mill Place	C2
Mair Street	C2	Mill Street	C2
Mill Court	E2	Old School Wynd	B3
Mill Crescent	E2	Poole Avenue	B2
Mill Road	E2	Stewart Avenue	B2
Murdoch Nisbet	D2		
Court			

Index to Newmilns

Index to Sorn

Alstonpapple	F2	Campbell Street	E2	Mure Place	B2	
Baldies Brae	C2	Castle Street	D2	Nelson Street	C2	Anderson Crescent	B1
Borebrae	C2	Clearmount Avenue	C2	Persian Sands	D2	Dalgain Drive	C2
Borebrae Crescent	C1	Cochrane Place (4)	E2	Queens Crescent	B2	Dalyearnoch Road	B1
Braehead Road	D2	Covenanters Court (1)	C2	Regents Court	C2	Fir Park	B1
Bridgend	D2	Craigview Road (2)	D2	Riverbank Street	C2	Main Street	C2
Brown Street	B2	Dalwhatswood Road	E1	Shields Road	C2	Old Avenue	B2
Browns Road	D2	Darnleyhill Walk	C2	Stoneygate Road	B3	Treebank Cottages	B1
Burn Road	D2	Darvel Road	E2	Strath Crescent	B3	Woodlands Road	C1
Campbell Court	E2	Drygate Street	D2	Stratholm Terrace	A3	Woolmill Place	C2
		Drygatehead	D1				
		East Church Court	D1				

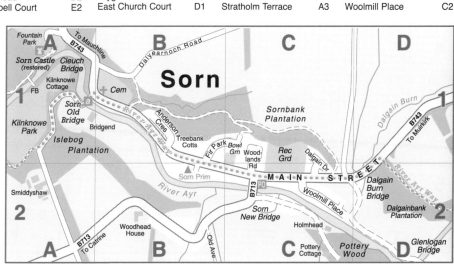

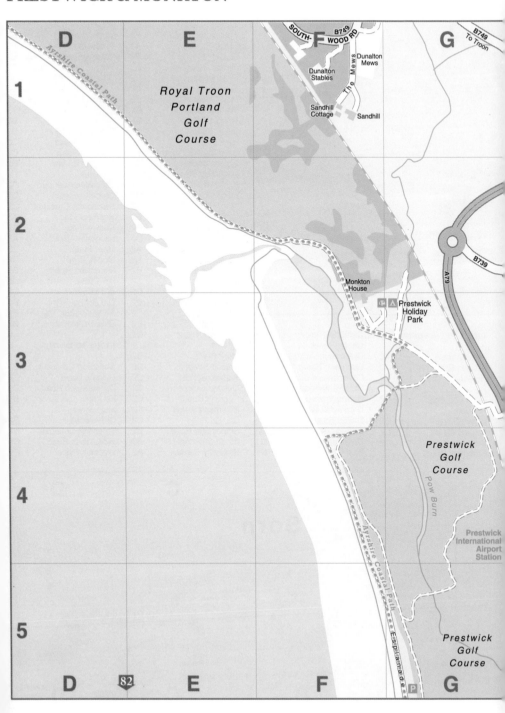

D
E
F
G

1

Ayrshire Coastal Path

SOUTH-WOOD RD
B749

B749
To Troon

Dunalton
Mews

Dunalton
Stables

The Mews

Royal Troon
Portland
Golf
Course

Sandhill
Cottage

Sandhill

2

B739

A79

Monkton
House

Prestwick
Holiday
Park

3

Prestwick
Golf
Course

Pow Burn

4

Ayrshire Coastal Path

Prestwick
International
Airport
Station

5

Esplanade

Prestwick
Golf
Course

D
82
E
F
G

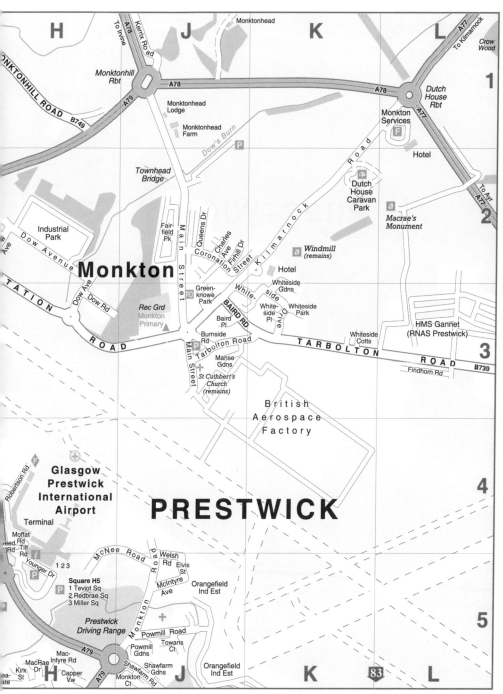

Index to street names can be found starting on page 94

PRESTWICK

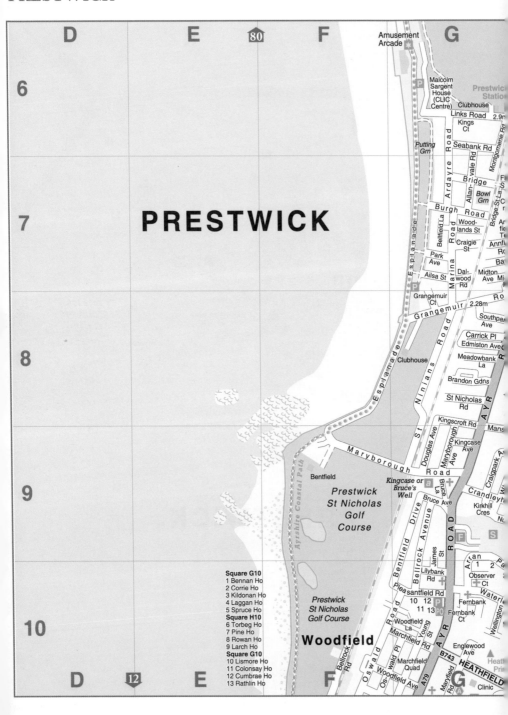

PRESTWICK

Amusement Arcade

Malcolm Sargent House (CLIC Centre)

Prestwick Station

Clubhouse

Links Road 2.9m

Kings Ct

Putting Grn

Seabank Rd

Ardayre Road

Allanvale Rd

Bridge

Bowl Grn

Burgh Road

Belfield La

Woodlands St

Craigie St

Park Ave

Dalwood Rd

Ailsa St

Midton Ave

Grangemuir Ct

Grangemuir 2.28m

Road

Southpark Ave

Carrick Pl

Edmiston Ave

Esplanade

Meadowbank La

Clubhouse

Brandon Gdns

St Ninians Road

St Nicholas Rd

Kingscroft Rd

Mans

Douglas Ave

Maryborough Ave

Kingcase Ave

Maryborough

Road

Bentfield

Kingcase or Bruce's Well

Craigpark

Cranleyh

Bruce Ave

Kirkhill Cres

Ayrshire Coastal Path

Prestwick St Nicholas Golf Course

Bentfield Drive

Bellrock Avenue

James St

AYR ROAD

Arran

Observer

Lilybank Rd

Pleasantfield Rd

Fernbank

Prestwick St Nicholas Golf Course

10 12

11 13

Fernbank Ct

Woodfield La

Young St

Marchfield Rd

Englewood Ave

Woodfield

Bellrock Rd

Oswald

Marchfield Quad

Marchfield Rd

B743 HEATHFIELD

A79

Woodfield Ave

Clinic

Square G10
1 Bennan Ho
2 Corrie Ho
3 Kildonan Ho
4 Laggan Ho
5 Spruce Ho
Square H10
6 Torbeg Ho
7 Pine Ho
8 Rowan Ho
9 Larch Ho
Square G10
10 Lismore Ho
11 Colonsay Ho
12 Cumbrae Ho
13 Rathlin Ho

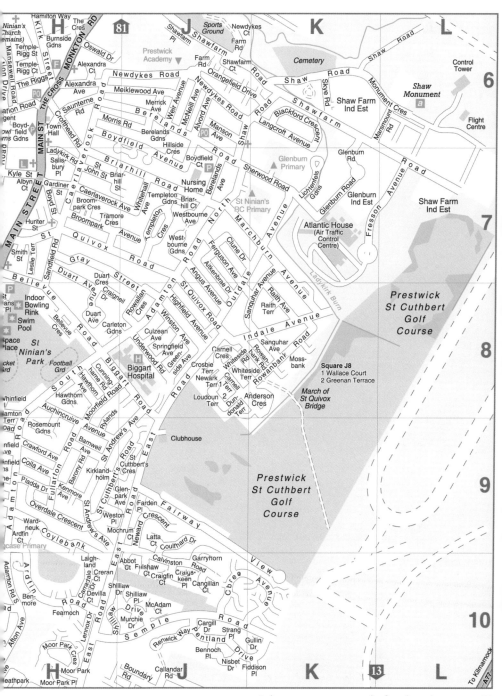

Index to street names can be found starting on page 94

PATNA & SKELMORLIE

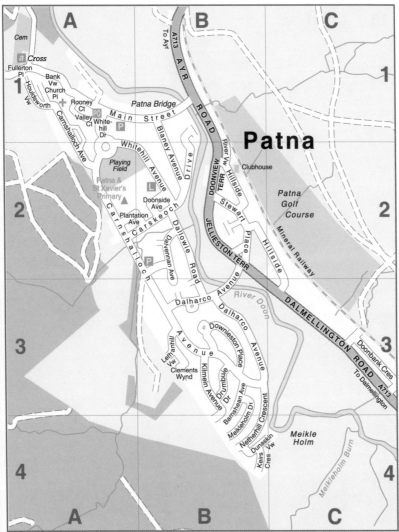

Index to Patna

Ayr Road	B1	Dalvennan Avenue	B2	Lethanhill View	B3
Bank View	A1	Doonbank Crescent	C3	Main Street	A1
Barnshean Avenue	B3	Doonside Avenue	B2	Meikleholm Drive	B4
Blaney Avenue	B1	Doonview Terrace	B2	Netherhill Crescent	B4
Carnshalloch Avenue	A2	Downieston Place	B3	Plantation Avenue	A2
Carskeoch Drive	B2	Drumbuie Drive	B3	River View	B2
Church Place	A1	Dunaskin View	B4	Rooney Court	A1
Clements Wynd	B3	Fullerton Place	A1	Stewart Place	B2
Dalharco Avenue	B3	Hillside	B2	Valley Court	A1
Dallowie Road	B2	Houldsworth View	A1	Whitehill Avenue	A2
Dalmellington Road	C3	Jellieston Terrace	B2	Whitehill Drive	A1
		Keirs Crescent	B4		
		Kilmein Avenue	B3		

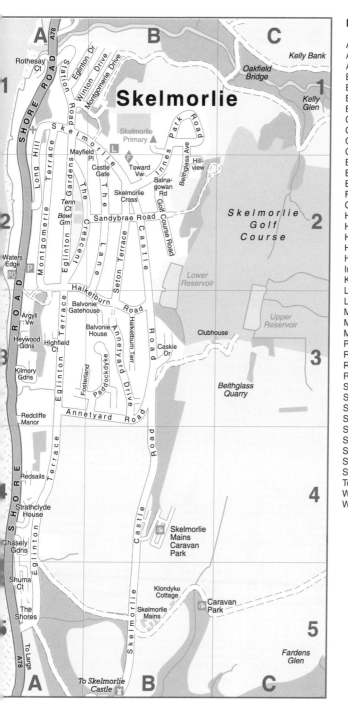

Index to Skelmorlie

Annetyard Drive	B3
Annetyard Road	B3
Argyll View	A3
Balnagowan Road	B2
Balvonie Gatehouse	A3
Balvonie House	B3
Beithglass Avenue	B2
Caskie Drive	B3
Castle Gate	B2
Chasely Gardens	A4
Crescent, The	A2
Eglinton Drive	A1
Eglinton Gardens	A2
Eglinton Terrace	A3, A4
Fosterland	A3
Golf Course Road	B2
Halketburn Road	B3
Halketburn Terrace	B3
Heywood Gardens	A3
Highfield Court	A3
Hillview	B2
Innes Park Road	B2
Kilmory Gardens	A3
Lane, The	B2
Long Hill	A2
Mayfield Place	A1
Montgomerie Drive	B1
Montgomerie Terrace	A2
Paddockdyke	B3
Redcliffe Manor	A3
Redsails	A4
Rothesay Court	A1
Sandybrae Road	B2
Seton Terrace	B2
Shore Road	A1, A4
Shores, The	A5
Shuma Court	A5
Skelmorlie Castle Road	A1, B5
Skelmorlie Cross	B2
Station Road	A1
Strathclyde House	A4
Toward View	B2
Waters Edge	A2
Winton Drive	A1

STEWARTON & SYMINGTON

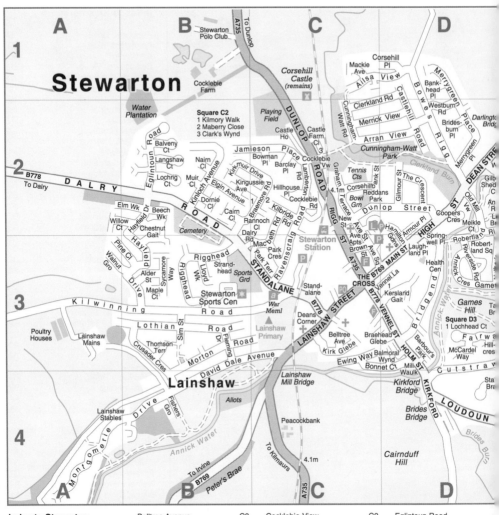

Index to Stewarton

Ailsa View	C1	Belltree Avenue	C3	Cocklebie View	C2	Eglintoun Road
Albert Avenue	E2	Bonnet Court	C3	Coopers Crescent	D2	Elgin Avenue
Albert Court	E2	Bowes Rigg	D1	Corsehillbank Street	C2	Elm Walk
Albert Place	E2	Bowman Place	C2	Corsehill Place	D1	Ewing Way
Albert Wynd	E2	Braehead Glebe	C3	Crusader Crescent	B3	Fairways
Alder Street	B3	Braemore Road	C2	Crescent, The	D2	Fishers Grove
Annick Bank	E1	Bridesburn Place	D2	Cross, The	C3	Fleming Drive
Annick Crescent	D3	Bridgend	D3	Cunningham Watt	C2	Gameshill View
Annick Rise	D2	Brown Street	C3	Road		Gilbert Sheddon
Armour Place	D2	Burnbank Place	E2	Cutsburn Brae	E3	Court
Arran View	C2	Burnbridge Wynd	E2	Cutsburn Place	E3	Gilmour Street
Avenue Apartments	C3	Cairn Close	B2	Cutsburn Road	E3	Golf Loan
Avenue Square	C3	Cairnduff Place	E2	Cutstraw Road	D4	Graham Terrace
Avenue Street	C2	Canmore Place	E2	Dalry Road	A2	Hamilton Gardens
Balmoral Wynd	D3	Castle Farm Close	C2	Darlington View	E2	Hayfield Drive	B2
Balveny Court	B2	Castle House	C2	David Dale Avenue	B4	High Street
Bankhead Place	D1	Castlehill Road	D2	Dean Street	D2	Hillcrest
Barbours Park	D3	Cauldhame Rigg	E3	Deans Corner	C3	Hillhouse Place
Barclay Place	C2	Chestnut Gait	B2	Dornie Close	B2	Holmhead Drive
Beech Walk	B2	Clark's Wynd (3)	C2	Draffen Mount	E4	Holm Street
		Clerkland Road	C2	Dunlop Road	C2	Jamieson Place
		Cocklebie Road	C2	Dunlop Street	C2	Jubilee Drive

TARBOLTON & TROON

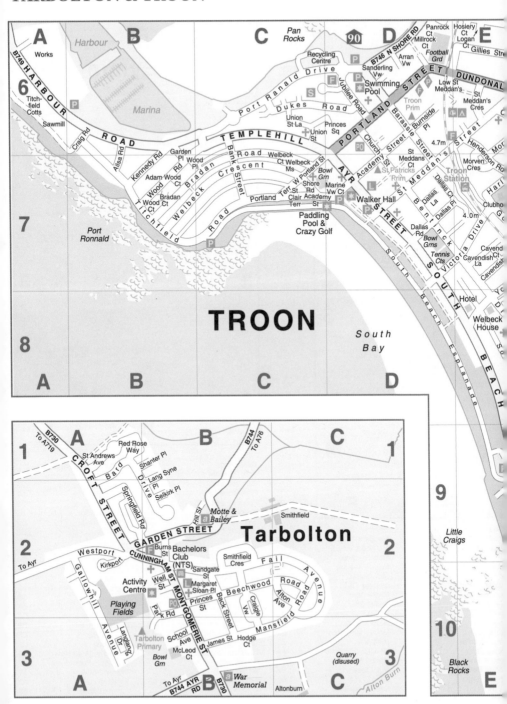

TROON

South Bay

Tarbolton

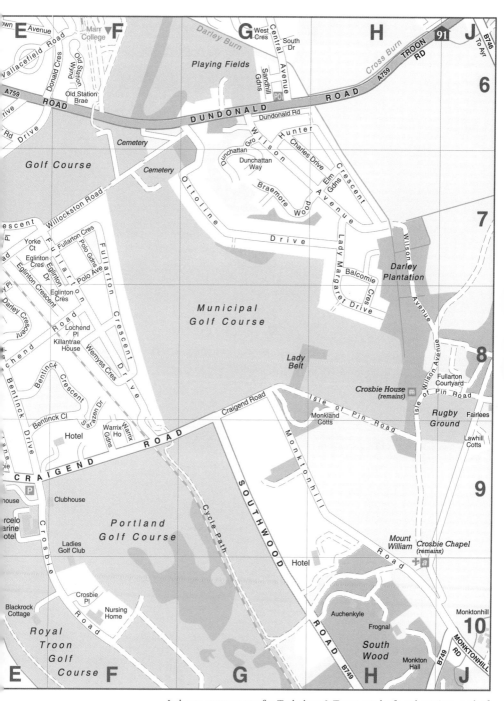

Index to street names for Tarbolton & Troon can be found starting overleaf

TROON & BARASSIE

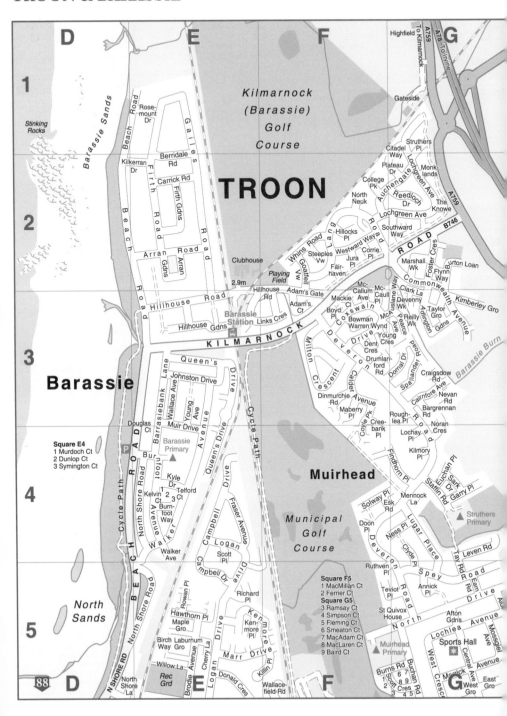

Square E4
1 Murdoch Ct
2 Dunlop Ct
3 Symington Ct

Square F5
1 MacMillan Ct
2 Ferrier Ct
Square G5
3 Ramsay Ct
4 Simpson Ct
5 Fleming Ct
6 Smeaton Ct
7 MacAdam Ct
8 MacLaren Ct
9 Baird Ct

Index to Tarbolton

Alton Avenue	C2
Ayr Road	B3
Back Street	B2
Bard Drive	A1
Beechwood Road	B2
Burns Street	B2
Craigie View	B2
Croft Street	A1
Cunningham Street	A2
Fail Avenue	B2
Gallowhill Avenue	A2
Garden Street	A2
Hill Street	B2
Hodge Court	B3
James Street	B3
Kirkport	A2
Langlands Drive	A3
Lang Syne Place	B1
Mcleod Court	B3
Mansefield Road	B3
Margaret Sloan Place	B2
Montgomerie Street	B2
Park Road	B2
Princes Street	B2
Red Rose Way	A1
St Andrews Avenue	A1
Sandgate Street	B2
School Avenue	B3
Selkirk Place	B2
Shanter Place	B1
Smithfield Crescent	B2
Springfield Road	A2
Well Street	B2
Westport	A2

Index to Troon

Academy Street	D7
Adam Wood Court	B7
Adams Court	F3
Adam's Gate	F3
Adlington Gardens	G3
Afton Gardens	G5
Ailsa Road	B7
Aldersyde Avenue	G5
Annick Place	G5
Arran Gardens	E2
Arran Road	E2
Arran View	D6
Auchengate	F2
Ayr Street	D7
Baird Court (9)	G5
Balcomie Crescent	H7
Bank Street	C7
Barassie Street	D6
Barassiebank Lane	E4
Bargrennan Road	G3
Beach Road	D1, D5
Beechwood Paddock	J5
Bentinck Close	E9
Bentinck Crescent	E8
Bentinck Drive	D7, E8
Berriedale Road	E2
Birch Way	E5
Bowman Warren Wynd	F3
Boyd Place	F3

Bradan Court	B7
Bradan Road	B7
Braemore Wood	G7
Brodie Avenue	E5
Brown Avenue	E6
Buchan Road	G5
Burnfoot Avenue	E4
Burnfoot Way	E4
Burns Road	F5
Burnside Place	D6
Burton Loan	G2
Cairnfore Avenue	G3
Calder Avenue	F3
Campbell Drive	E4
Carrick Road	E2
Cavendish Court	E7
Cavendish Lane	E7
Cavendish Place	E7
Central Avenue	G5, G6
Cessnock Road	E6
Chapelhill Cottages	H2
Charles Drive	G6
Cherry Lane	E5
Church Street	D6
Citadel Way	G1
Clark Lane	G2
Clyde Place	G4
College Park	F2
Collenan Avenue	H5
Collins Road	H5
Commonwealth Avenue	G2
Corrie Place	F2
Coxswain Drive	F3
Coyle Park	F4
Craig Road	B6
Craigend Road	E9, G8
Craigsdow Road	G3
Craiksland Place	H5
Craiksland Road	J5
Creebank Place	F4
Crosbie Court	E9
Crosbie Place	F10
Crosbie Road	E9
Crossburn Drive	J5
Crossburn Lane	J5
Crossburn Terrace	J5
Crummieholm Gardens	H5
Dallas Court	D7
Dallas Lane	D7
Dallas Place	D7
Dallas Road	D7
Darley Crescent	E8
Darley Place	E8
Dent Crescent	F3
Devenny Walk	G3
Deveron Road	F3, F4
Dinmurchie Road	F3
Donald Crescent	E5, E6
Doon Place	F4
Dornal Drive	G3
Douglas Court	E3
Drumlanford Road	F3
Dukes Road	C6
Dunchattan Grove	G7
Dunchattan Way	G7
Dundonald Road	E6, G6
Dunlop Court (2)	E4
continued overleaf...	

TURNBERRY & WEST KILBRIDE

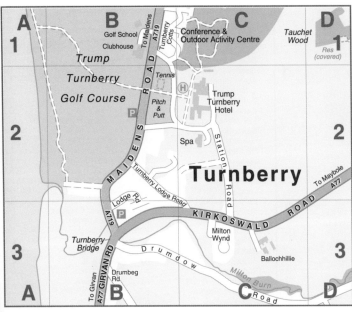

Index to Troon
continued from overleaf...

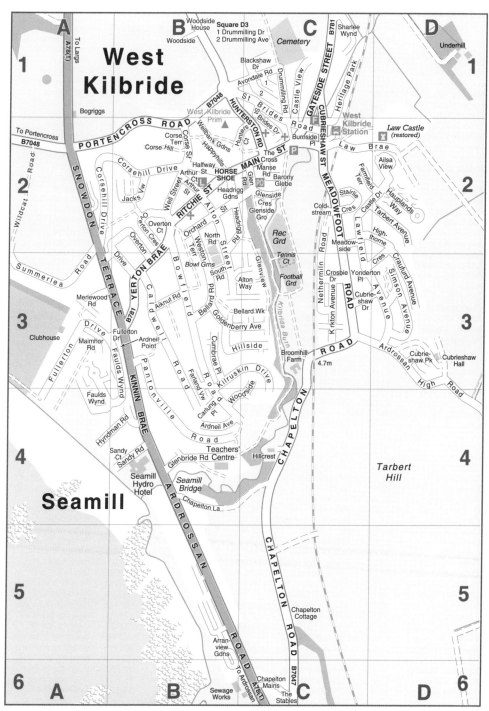

Index to Turnberry

Drumbeg Road	92 B3
Drumdow Road	92 B3
Girvan Road	92 B3
Kirkoswald Road	92 C3
Lodge Road	92 B2
Maidens Road	92 B2
Milton Wynd	92 C3
Station Road	92 C2
Turnberry Cottages	92 B1
Turnberry Lodge	92 B2
Road	

Index to West Kilbride

Aiknut Road	93 B3
Ailsa View	93 D2
Alton Street	93 B2
Alton Way	93 C3
Ardneil Avenue	93 B4
Ardneil Point	93 B3
Ardrossan High Road	93 D3
Ardrossan Road	93 B4
Arranview Gardens	93 B5
Arthur Court	93 B2
Arthur Street	93 B2
Avondale Road	93 C1
Bank Cottages	93 C6
Barony Glebe	93 C2
Bellard Road	93 B3
Bellard Walk	93 C3
Blackshaw Drive	93 C1
Bowfield Road	93 B3
Burnside Place	93 C2
Caldwell Road	93 B3
Carlung Place	93 B4
Castle Drive	93 C2
Castle View	93 C1
Chapelton Cottage	93 C5
Chapelton Lane	93 C5
Chapelton Mains	93 C6
Chapelton Road	93 C4, C5
Coldstream	93 C2
Corse Hill	93 B2
Corse Street	93 B2
Corse Terrace	93 B2
Corsehill Drive	93 A2, B2
Craufurd Avenue	93 D3
Crosbie Drive	93 C3
Cross, The	93 C2
Cubrieshaw Drive	93 C3
Cubrieshaw Park	93 D3
Cubrieshaw Street	93 C2
Cumbrae Place	93 B3
Drummilling	93 C1
Avenue (2)	
Drummilling	93 C1
Drive (1)	
Drummilling Road	93 C1
Farland View	93 B3
Farmfield Terrace	93 C2
Faulds Wynd	93 A4, B3
Fullerton Drive	93 A3

Gateside Street	93 C1
Glen Road	93 C2
Glenbride Road	93 B4
Glenside Crescent	93 C2
Glenside Grove	93 C2
Glenview	93 C3
Goldenberry	93 B3
Avenue	
Halfway Street	93 B2
Happyhills	93 B2
Hauplands Way	93 D2
Headrigg Gardens	93 B2
Headrigg Road	93 B2
Heritage Park	93 C1
Highthorne Crescent	93 D2
Hillside	93 B3
Horse Shoe	93 B2
Hunters Court	93 B2
Hunterston Road	93 B1
Hyndman Road	93 A4
Jacks View	93 B2
Kilruskin Drive	93 B3
Kinnin Brae	93 B3
Kirkton Avenue	93 C3
Law Brae	93 C2
Lawfield Avenue	93 C2
Maimhor Road	93 A3
Main Street	93 C2
Manse Road	93 C2
Meadowfoot Road	93 C2
Meadowside	93 C2
Merlewood Road	93 A3
Nethermiln Road	93 C3
North Road	93 B2
Orchard Street	93 B2
Overton Court	93 B2
Overton Crescent	93 B2
Overton Drive	93 B2
Pantonville Road	93 B4
Portencross Road	93 A2
Ritchie Street	93 B2
St Brides Drive	93 C1
St Brides Road	93 C1
Sandy Court	93 B4
Sandy Road	93 B4
Sharlee Wynd	93 C1
Simson Avenue	93 D3
Snowdon Terrace	93 A2
South Road	93 B3
Stables, The	93 C6
Stairlie Crescent	93 C2
Summerlea Road	93 A3
Tarbert Avenue	93 D2
Well Street	93 B2
Wellbank Gardens	93 B2
Weston Terrace	93 B2
Wildcat Road	93 A2
Woodside	93 B4
(Seamill)	
Woodside	93 B1
(West Kilbride)	
Woodside House	93 B1
Yerton Brae	93 B3
Yonderton Place	93 C3

Index to Ayr, Alloway, Prestwick & Monkton

Abbot Court	83 J10
Abbots	12 A21
Crescent	
Abbots Way	12 A21, B20
Abercromby	16 C19
Drive	
Academy Street	14 E14
Adamton Road	83 J8
North	
Adamton Road	83 H9, H10
South	
Adamton Terrace	83 H8
Afton Avenue	83 H10
Afton Court	15 G17
Ailsa Place	14 D14
Ailsa Street	82 G7
Ailsa View	12 A21
Ailsa View	12 A21
Gardens	
Ailsa View Place	12 A21
Ailsa View Wynd	12 A21
Airlie Court	14 D17
Aitkenbrae Drive	83 J7
Albert Terrace	14 F15
Albyn Court	83 H7
Alder Bank	15 J17
Alderston Avenue	12 F12
Alderston Park	12 F12
Alderston Place	12 F12
Alexandra Avenue	83 H6
Alexandra Court	83 H6
Alexandra Terrace	12 F12
Allan Place	13 H12
Allanvale Road	82 G7
Allenfield Road	15 J17
Allison Street	12 F13
Alloway	16 D22
Alloway Park	14 D15
Alloway Place	14 D16
Alloway Place	14 D15
Lane	
Alloway Street	14 E16
Alton House	17 J21
Altry Place	12 A22
Alvord Avenue	83 J6
Anderson Crescent	17 G19
(Ayr)	
Anderson Crescent	83 K8
(Prestwick)	
Angus Avenue	83 J7
Annfield Glen Road	17 G19
Annfield Road	82 G7
Annfield Terrace	82 G7
Annpit Road	12 G11
Ardayre Road	82 G7
Ardfin Court	83 H9
Ardfin Road	83 H10
Ardlui Road	12 F11
Argyle Park	12 F13
Armour Drive	15 H17
Arnprior Place	16 E21

Arran Mall	14 E1
Arran Park	12 G1
Arran Terrace	14 D1
Arranview Court	12 G·
Arrol Drive	14 C1
Arrol Drive	16 C1
Arrol Park	14 D1
Arthur Street	14 E·
Ashgrove Street	14 F1
Aspen Court	15 J·
Aspen Road	15 J·
Auchenbeg	17 F:
Crescent	
Auchendoon	14 C·
Crescent	
Auchendoon	16 C·
Crescent	
Auchentrae	14 C
Crescent	
Auchentrae	16 C
Crescent	
Auchincruive	83 I
Avenue	
Auld Nick's View	16 D.
Ayr Road	82 G8, (
Ayr Road	82 G
Back Hawkhill	12 G
Avenue	
Back Main Street	12 E
Back Peebles Street	12 E.
Baird Place	81
Baird Road	16 D
(Alloway)	
Baird Road	81
(Monkton)	
Ballantine Drive	14 E
Ballantine Drive	14 E
Lane	
Balminnoch Park	16 B
Bank Street	82 ·
Bankfield Park	17 H
Barnford Crescent	17 F
Barns Court	14 E
Barns Crescent	14 E
Barns Park	14 E
Barns Street	14 E
Barns Street Lane	14 E
Barns Terrace	14 E
Barns Terrace Lane	14 E
Barnweil Avenue	83
Barony Road	83
Bath Place	14 [
Bathurst Drive	17 F
Beagle Crescent	16 E
Beech Grove	15 F
Belleisle Cottages	16 (
Belleisle Drive	16 (
Belleisle Wynd	16 (
Bellesleyhill Avenue	12 (
Bellesleyhill Court	12 I
Bellesleyhill Road	12 I
Bellevale Avenue	14 E
Bellevale Quadrant	14 E
Bellevue Cottages	14 I

ellevue Crescent (Ayr)	14 E16	Bridge Street Lane	82 G7	
ellevue Crescent (Prestwick)	83 H8	Britannia Place	12 G12	
ellevue Lane	14 E16	Broadwood Park	17 F22	
ellevue Road (Ayr)	14 D16	Broomfield Garden	14 E17	
ellevue Road (Prestwick)	83 H7	Broomfield Road	14 E17	
ellevue Street	14 E16	Broompark Avenue	83 H7	
ellfield Lane	82 G7	Broompark Crescent	83 H7	
ellrock Avenue	12 G10	Broun Drive	16 D22	
ellrock Road	12 F11	Browncarrick Drive	12 A22	
elmont Avenue	14 F18	Bruce Avenue	82 G9	
elmont Crescent	14 F18	Bruce Crescent	14 D15	
elmont Drive	14 F18	Bruce Lane	82 G9	
elmont Place East	14 F17	Buchan Court (4)	12 D14	
elmont Place West	14 F17	Burgh Road	82 G7	
elmont Road	14 F18	Burnbank Place	17 G19	
elvidere Terrace	12 F13	Burnbank Road	17 G19	
enmore	83 H10	Burness Avenue	16 E21	
ennan House (1)	12 G10	Burnett Terrace	12 G14	
ennoch Place	83 J10	Burns Statue Square	14 E16	
entfield Avenue	14 D17	Burns' Wicket	16 D22	
entfield Drive	12 G10	Burnside Gardens	83 H6	
relands Avenue	83 J7	Burnside Road	81 J3	
relands Gardens	83 J6	Caerlaverock Avenue	83 H7	
relands Road	83 J6	Caerlaverock Road	83 H7	
resford Court	14 E16	Cairn Crescent	16 C21	
resford Lane	14 E16	Cairnsmore Drive	16 B22	
resford Terrace	14 E16	Caledonia Road	15 H17	
jgart Road	83 H8	Callander Road	83 J10	
ch Road	17 H19	Callendar Place	12 G11	
ackburn Drive	14 C17	Calvinston Road	83 J10	
ackburn Place	14 D17	Cambusdoon Drive	16 D21	
ackburn Road	14 D17	Cambuslea Gardens	12 G12	
ackford Crescent	83 K6	Cambuslea Road	12 G12	
ackfriars Court	14 E15	Campbell Court	15 H15	
ackfriars Walk	14 E15	Campbell Street	12 F12	
ackhill Street	15 G18	Camphill Place	15 G18	
ackhouse Place	15 H15	Campion Court	17 G20	
anefield Avenue	83 H9	Cangillan Court	83 J10	
aebell Grove	13 L13	Capper View	81 H5	
at Vennal	12 E14	Carcluie Crescent	17 G20	
aswell Park	14 E15	Cargill Drive	83 J10	
undary Road	13 J11	Carleton Gardens	83 H8	
urtree Park	14 F17	Carnell Crescent	83 J8	
awman Road	14 F17	Carnell Terrace	83 J8	
yd Street	83 H7	Carradale Drive	83 H10	
ydfield Avenue	83 H6	Carrick Avenue	14 E17	
ydfield Court	83 J7	Carrick Gardens	14 E17	
ydfield Gardens	83 H6	Carrick Park	14 E17	
acken Park	17 H20	Carrick Place	82 G8	
adan Drive	17 G21	Carrick Road	14 E17	
aehead Avenue	13 H13	Carrick Road Lane	14 E17	
aehead Crescent	13 H13	Carrick Street	14 E15	
aemar Square	13 J13	Carseloch Road	16 E22	
aeside Road	13 J13	Carwinshoch View	14 C18	
andon Gardens	82 G8	Cassillis Street	14 D15	
ar Grove	17 H19	Castle Square	12 A20	
arhill Court	83 J7	Castle View	12 A20	
arhill Road	83 H7	Castle Walk	12 B20	
arhill Street	83 H7	Castlehill Court	15 G18	
dge Street	82 G7			

Castlehill Crescent	14 F17	Craigskeen Place	83 J10
Castlehill Gardens	15 H18	Craigstewart Crescent	16 B22
Castlehill Road	14 F17	Craigston Avenue	15 H17
Cathcart Street	12 E14	Craigweil Place	14 D16
Cedar Road	15 J18	Craigweil Road	14 D16
Cedar Road	17 H19	Crandleyhill Road	82 G9
Celandine Bank	17 H20	Cranesbill Court	17 G20
Cessnock Place	15 H17	Crawford Avenue	83 H9
Chalmers Avenue	14 F18	Creran Court	83 H10
Chalmers Road	14 E17	Crescent, The	83 H6
Chapelpark Road	14 E18	Crocus Bank	17 H20
Chapelton Crescent	16 E23	Crofthead Road (Ayr)	15 J18
Charles Avenue	81 J2	Crofthead Road (Prestwick)	83 H6
Charlotte Street	14 D15	Cromwell Road	12 D14
Charlotte Street Lane	14 D15	Crosbie Terrace	83 J8
Cherry Blossom Way	13 L13	Cross Gait	12 F14
Cherry Hill Road	17 G21	Cross Street	12 E14
Chestnut Road	15 J17	Cross, The	83 H6
Church Court	12 F14	Crossburn	12 A22
Churchill Crescent	15 H15	Crown Square	12 E13
Churchill Tower	12 D13	Crown Street	12 E13
Citadel Place	12 D14	Culzean Avenue	83 J8
Clarendon Place	15 H18	Culzean Road	16 C20
Clarke Avenue	14 D17	Cumbrae Drive	12 A21
Clochranhill Road	16 E21	Cumbrae House (12)	12 G10
Cloverhill	15 J17	Cunning Park Drive	16 C20
Clune Drive	83 J7	Cunningham Crescent	15 G17
Cochrane Place	82 G7	Cunningham Place	15 H17
Coila Avenue	83 H9	Cunninghame Road	83 H8
Colonsay House (11)	12 G10	Curtican Place	14 E17
Content Avenue	14 F15	Daisy Cottages	12 F12
Content Court	17 J21	Daisy Place	13 L13
Content Street	12 F14	Dalblair Arcade	14 E15
Coranbae Place	12 A22	Dalblair Court	14 E15
Cornhill	17 G20	Dalblair Road	14 E15
Coronation Street	81 J2	Dalblair Way	14 E16
Corrie House (2)	12 G10	Dalmellington Road	15 G18
Corsehill Park	14 E18	Dalmellington Road	17 H19
Corsehill Place	14 E18	Dalmilling Crescent	13 J14
Corsehill Road	14 E18	Dalmilling Drive	13 J13
Corserine Road	12 A22	Dalmilling Road	13 J13
Corton Howe	17 F23	Dalton Park	12 A21
Corton Lea	17 F23	Dalwood Road	82 G7
Corton Shaw	17 G23	Damside	12 E13
Coulthard Drive	83 J9	Davidson Place	12 F14
Cow Wynd	14 E15	Devilla Court	83 H10
Cowan Crescent	13 H12	Dongola Road	14 F17
Coylebank	83 H9	Donnini Court (1)	12 D14
Craig Drive	12 A21	Doon Avenue	12 G10
Craigfin Court	83 J10	Doon Avenue	83 H10
Craighall Place	17 F21	Doonbank Park	16 C23
Craigholm Road	15 J16	Doonfoot Road	14 D18
Craigie Avenue	14 F15	Doonfoot Road	16 C20
Craigie Lea	15 G15	Doonholm Park	16 E22
Craigie Road	12 G14	Doonholm Park	17 F23
Craigie Street	82 G7	Doonholm Place	16 E22
Craigie Walk	15 H16	Doonholm Road	16 D22
Craigie Way	15 G15	Doonholm Road	17 F23
Craigneil Drive	83 H8		
Craigpark Avenue	82 G9		
Craigshiel Place	16 C19		

Index to Ayr, Prestwick & Monkton

Doonvale Drive 17 F23
Doonvale Place 17 F23
Doonview Gardens 16 B21
Doonview Wynd 16 B21
Dornoch Park 14 D17
Douglas Avenue 82 G9
Douglas Lane 14 E15
Douglas Street 14 E15
Dow Avenue 81 H2, H3
Dow Road 81 H2
Drumellan Road 17 F21
Drummond Crescent 13 K13
Duart Avenue 83 H7
Duart Crescent 83 H7
Duke Terrace 12 F13
Dumfries Park 17 F22
Dunalton Mews 80 F1
Dunalton Stables 80 F1
Dundonald Terrace 83 J8
Dunlop Crescent 13 K14
Dunlop Terrace 15 J14
Dunure Road 12 A22
Dunure Road 16 B21
Dutch Mill 16 D23
Earls Way 12 B20
East Park Road 12 G12
East Road 13 H11
East Road 83 J9
Edenhall Road 12 G11
Edmiston Avenue 82 G8
Eglinton Place 12 D14
Eglinton Terrace 12 D14
Elba Court 12 F14
Elba Street 12 F14
Ellisland Place 15 G17
Ellisland Square 15 G17
Elmbank Street 12 E12
Elms Way 12 G11
Elvis Street 81 J5
Englewood Avenue 12 G10
Esplanade (Ayr) 12 D14
Esplanade (Ayr) 14 C17
Esplanade (Ayr) 14 D15
Esplanade (Ayr) 16 C19
Esplanade (Prestwick) 80 G5
Esplanade (Prestwick) 82 F8
Esplanade (Prestwick) 82 G7
Ettrick Place 12 G11
Ewenfield Avenue 14 E18
Ewenfield Gardens 17 F19
Ewenfield Park 16 E19
Ewenfield Place 17 F19
Ewenfield Road 16 E19
Fairfield Park (Ayr) 14 D16
Fairfield Park (Prestwick) 81 J2
Fairfield Road 14 D16
Fairway View 83 J9
Falkland Park Road 12 F12
Falkland Place 12 F12

Falkland Road 12 F12
Farden Place 83 J9
Farm Road 83 J6
Farrell Place 12 G13
Fearnoch 83 H10
Fellhill Street 15 G18
Fenwickland Avenue 17 F19
Fenwickland Place 17 F19
Ferguson Avenue 83 J7
Ferguson Street 13 H13
Fern Brae 17 H20
Fernbank 12 G10
Fernbank Court 12 G10
Fiddison Place 13 K10
Findhorn Road 81 L3
Finlas Avenue 17 G20
Finnick Glen 17 F20
Fir Bank 15 H18
Firhill Drive 81 J2
Flaxton Court 14 E17
Forbes Drive 13 H11
Forehill Road 15 G17
Forest Way 15 H18
Forge Road 12 G11
Fort Court 12 E14
Fort Street 14 E15
Fotheringham Road 14 F15
Foxglove Place 17 H20
Fresson Avenue 83 K7
Fullarton Road 83 H9
Fullarton Street 14 E15
Fulshaw Court 83 J10
Fulshaw Crescent 13 L13
Fulshaw Place 13 K12
Galloway Avenue 13 H13
Galloway Gardens 13 H13
Garden Court 12 E14
Garden Street 12 E14
Gardiner Street 83 H7
Garryhorn 83 J10
Gartferry Court 14 D17
Gavin Hamilton Court 15 H17
Gearholm Road 16 C20
Gemmell Court 13 H14
Gemmell Crescent 13 H14
George Place 12 A21
George Square 12 F14
George Street 12 F14
George's Avenue 12 G12
Glebe Crescent 12 E13
Glebe Road 12 E13
Glenalla Crescent 16 B22
Glenburn Road 83 K7
Glencairn Road 15 G17
Glenconner Place 15 G17
Glenconner Road 15 G17
Glendale Crescent 17 G19
Glendale Place 17 G19
Glendrissaig Drive 17 F23
Glenford Place 12 D14

Glengall Lane 17 G21
Glenmount Place 12 A22
Glenmuir Court 13 H13
Glenmuir Place 13 J12
Glenmuir Road 13 J13
Glenmuir Square 13 J13
Glenpark Avenue 83 J9
Glenpark Place 17 G20
Glenriddel Road 15 G17
Good Shepherd Court 13 J13
Gordon Street 12 F12
Gordon Terrace 14 F15
Gorse Park 17 H20
Goschen Terrace 12 G13
Goukscroft Court 16 C20
Goukscroft Park 16 C20
Gould Street 12 G13
Gowan Bank Road 17 G21
Gower Place 17 G20
Grange Avenue 17 G21
Grangemuir Court 82 G8
Grangemuir Road 82 G8
Gray Street 83 H7
Green Street 12 E14
Green Street Lane 12 E13
Greenan Grove 12 A20
Greenan Park 12 A20
Greenan Place 12 B20
Greenan Road 12 A20
Greenan Terrace (2) 83 J8
Greenan Way 12 A20
Greenfield Avenue 16 C20
Greenknowe Park 81 J3
Greenside Avenue 83 J8
Greentree Park 17 H19
Guiltreehill 17 F22
Gullin Drive 83 K10
Halls Vennal 12 E13
Hamilton Crescent 14 F17
Hamilton Way 83 H6
Harebell Place 17 G20
Hartfield Road 14 E18
Harthall 13 K13
Hawkhill Avenue 12 G13
Hawthorn Avenue 83 H8
Hawthorn Drive 17 H19
Hawthorn Gardens 83 H8
Hay Hill 15 J15
Hazelwood Road 14 E17
Heather Park 17 H20
Heathfield Road (Ayr) 13 K12
Heathfield Road (Prestwick) 82 G10
Heathpark 83 H10
High Maybole Road 16 D23
High Road 13 K12
High Street 12 E14
High Street 14 E15
High Thorneyflat Wynd 13 K12
Highfield Avenue 83 J8
Highfield Drive 13 K12

Highfield Road 17 G
Hilary Crescent 14 F
Hillfoot Crescent 15 G
Hillfoot Road 15 G
Hillside Crescent 83
Hilltop Place 15 J
Hollow Park 17 G
Hollow Park Court 17 G
Holly Bank 15 J
Holmston Crescent 15 H
Holmston Drive 15 H
Holmston Gardens 14 F
Holmston Road 15 G
Home Farm Road 17 F
Honeysuckle Park 17 G
Hope Street 12 E
Hunter Street 83
Hunter's Avenue 12 G
Hunter's Avenue 83 H
Indale Avenue 83
Inkerman Court (6) 12 D
Inverkar Road 14 F
Iris Court 17 H
Ivy Place 15 J
James Brown Avenue 13 J
James Campbell Road 15 G
James Street (Ayr) 12 F
James Street (Prestwick) 12 G
John Street 12 F
Juniper Green 15 J
Kenmore Avenue 83
Kerrix Road 81
Kerse Park 17 G
Kilbrandon Crescent 12 A
Kilbrandon Way 12 A
Kildonan House (3) 12 G
Killoch Place 14 F
Kilmarnock Road 81
Kilnbank Crescent 15
Kincaidston Drive 17 G
King Street 12
Kingcase Avenue 82
Kings Court (Ayr) 12
Kings Court (Prestwick) 82
Kings Park 13
Kings Park 13
Kings Park Crescent
Kings Park Drive 13
Kingscroft Road 82
Kintyre Avenue 12
Kintyre Park 12
Kirk Port 14
Kirk Street 81 H5, 83
Kirkhill 82
Kirkholm Crescent
Kirkholm Avenue 12
Kirklandholm 83
Knoll Park 16
Knowe, The 14
Knoweholm 16

Name	Ref
Kyle Court	14 F16
Kyle Street (Ayr)	14 E15
Kyle Street (Prestwick)	83 H7
Laburnum Road	15 H17
Ladykirk Road	83 H7
Laggan House (4)	12 G10
Laigh Mount	17 F22
Laighland	83 H10
Lamford Drive	16 B22
Landsdowne Road	12 F12
Langcroft Avenue	83 K6
Larch House (9)	83 H10
Larchwood Road	17 H19
Larghill Lane	15 G18
Latta Court	83 J9
Laughlanglen Road	17 F21
Laurel Bank	17 H19
Lawson Street	12 G13
Leeward Park	17 F22
Lennox Drive	83 H10
Leslie Crescent	14 F17
Leslie Terrace	83 H7
Liberator Drive	13 K11
Lichtenfels Gardens	83 K7
Lilybank Road	12 G10
Limekiln Road	12 E12
Limonds Court	12 F14
Limonds Wynd	12 F14
Lindsay Street	13 H13
Lindston Place	17 F21
Linfern Place	17 G20
Links Road	82 G6
Lisburn Road	12 F11
Lismore House (10)	12 G10
Loaning, The	17 F21
Loch Park	12 B20
Lochlea Drive	15 G17
Lochside Court	12 G13
Lochside Road	12 G13
Lochside Road	13 H11
Longbank Drive	17 F19
Longbank Road	16 E19
Longhill Avenue	16 C23
Longhill Place	16 C23
Longlands Park	16 E19
Lorien Court	13 H11
Lorne Arcade	14 E15
Lothian Road	14 F16,
Lothian Road	15 G16
Loudon Terrace	83 J8
Loudoun House	17 J21
Low Road	13 K12
Lyath Walk	14 E15
Lugar Crescent	12 G10
Lymburn Place	15 G15
MacAdam Place	12 F14
MacAdam Square	12 F14
MacIntyre Road	81 H5
MacRae Drive	81 H5
McAdam Court	83 J10
McCall's Avenue	12 F12
McColgan Place	13 H12
McIntyre Avenue	81 J5
McLean Street	13 H13
McNairston Road	15 K18
McNee Road	81 H5
McNeill Avenue	83 J6
Main Road	13 J13
Main Street (Ayr)	12 E14
Main Street (Monkton)	81 J2, J3
Main Street (Prestwick)	83 H7
Mainholm Court	13 K14
Mainholm Crescent	15 J14
Mainholm Road	13 J13
Manse Gardens	81 J3
Mansewell Road	83 H6
Mansfield Road	82 G9
Manson Avenue	83 J6
Maple Drive	15 J18
Marchburn Avenue	83 K7
Marchfield Quadrant	12 F10
Marchfield Road	12 G10
Marchmont Road	14 E17
Marchmont Road Lane	14 E16
Marguerite Place	17 H20
Marigold Square	17 G20
Marina Road	82 G7
Marlborough Court (5)	12 D14
Marlepark	17 F20
Marsmount Road	83 K6
Martnaham Way	17 F23
Maryborough Avenue	82 G9
Maryborough Road	82 F9
Maryfield Place	12 G11
Maryfield Road	12 G11
Masonhill Place	15 H18
Masonhill Road	15 H17
Maybole Road	17 F20
Meadow Park	14 F18, G18
Meadow Park Drive	14 F18
Meadow Park Drive	15 G18
Meadowbank Lane	82 G8
Meiklewood Avenue	83 H6
Merkland Road	17 F21
Merrick Avenue	83 J6
Mews Lane	14 D15
Mews, The	80 F1
Midton Avenue	82 G7
Midton Road (Ayr)	14 E17
Midton Road 82 G7 (Prestwick)	
Midton Road (Prestwick)	83 H7
Mill Brae	14 F16
Mill Brae Court	14 F16
Mill Street	14 E15
Mill Wynd	14 E15
Miller Road	14 E16
Miller Square (3)	81 H5
Milton Park	17 G20
Mochrum Court	83 J9
Mochram Way	16 E23
Moffat Road	81 H4
Monkton Court	81 J5
Monkton Road	81 J5
Monkton Road	83 H6
Monktonhill Road	81 H1
Monkwood Place	17 F21
Montgomerie Road	82 G7
Montgomerie Terrace	12 D14
Monument Crescent	83 K6
Monument Road	14 E18
Monument Road	16 E20
Moor Park	83 H10
Moor Park Crescent	83 H10
Moor Park Place	83 H10
Moor Place	13 H11
Moor Road	13 H11
Moorfield Road	83 H8
Morris Road	83 H6
Morrison Gardens	15 G15
Morton Avenue	14 F18
Morton Road	14 F18
Mossbank	83 K8
Mossgiel Place	14 F17
Mossgiel Road	14 F17
Mosside Road	13 H11
Mote, The	17 F23
Mount Charles Crescent	16 C21
Mount Oliphant Crescent	14 F17
Mount Oliphant Place	15 G17
Mount, The	17 G19
Mountcharles	16 C21
Murchie Drive	83 J10
Murdoch's Lone	16 D22
Murray Place	13 H12
Murray Street	13 H13
Nelson Place	12 F13
New Bridge Street	12 E14
New Road	12 E13
Neward Crescent	83 J9
Newark Crescent	12 A22
Newark Terrace	83 J8
Newdykes Court	83 J6
Newdykes Road	83 J6
Newmarket Street	14 E15
Newton Park Court	12 G13
Nile Court	14 E15
Nisbet Drive	83 J10
Noltmire Road	13 H11
North Harbour Street	12 E14
Northdoon Place	16 C20
Northfield Avenue	12 F12
Northfield Court	12 F12
Northfield Place	12 F12
Northpark Avenue	12 G12
Nursery Avenue	82 G9
Nursery Grove	15 G18
Nursery Road	15 G18
Nursery Wynd	15 G18
Nurseryhall	13 J13
Oakwood Avenue	13 K13
Obree Avenue	83 J10
Observer Court	12 G10
Old Bridge Road	13 K12
Old Bridge Street	12 E14
Old Farm Road	13 J12
Old Hillfoot Road	15 G18
Orangefield Drive	83 J6
Orchard Avenue	15 G17
Orchard House	15 G17
Orchard Place	15 G17
Oswald Court	12 F12
Oswald Drive	83 H6
Oswald Lane	12 D13
Oswald Place	12 F10
Oswald Road	12 F10, F12
Outdale Avenue	83 J8
Overdale Crescent	83 H9
Overmills Crescent	15 J15
Overmills Road	15 J16
Park Avenue	82 G7
Park Circus	14 D16
Park Circus Lane	14 E16
Park Terrace	14 D15
Park View	16 E22
Parkhouse Street	14 E16
Paterson Street	12 G11
Pattle Place	16 E22
Pavilion Road	14 D15
Peebles Street	12 E13
Peggieshill Place	15 G18
Peggieshill Road	17 F19
Pemberton Valley	17 F21
Pentland Drive	83 J10
Philip Square	12 F14
Pine Brae	15 H18
Pine House (7)	83 H10
Pines, The	16 E22
Piperhill	17 F21
Pladda Drive	83 H9
Pleasantfield Road	12 G10
Poplar Way	15 J18
Portmark Avenue	16 B22
Powmill Gardens	81 J5
Powmill Road	81 J5
Prestwick Road	12 F12
Primrose Park	17 H20
Princess Court	12 F13
Promenade	12 F11
Quail Road	12 F11
Queen Street	12 F14
Queens Court	14 E15
Queens Drive	81 J2
Queens Quadrant	12 F14
Queens Terrace (Ayr)	14 D15
Queens Terrace (Prestwick)	82 G7

Index to Ayr, Prestwick, Monkton, Irvine, Dreghorn & Springside

Name	Ref
Queens Terrace	14 D15
Lane	
Racecourse Road	14 D17
Racecourse View	14 D18
Railway Cottages	16 E22
Raith Avenue	83 K8
Raith Terrace	83 K8
Raithill	17 G22
Rathlin House (13)	12 G10
Recawr Park	17 G20
Redbrae Square (2)	81 H5
Regent Park	83 H6
Renwick Way	83 J10
Riggs, The	83 H6
Rigwoodie Place	16 D22
River Ayr Walk	15 G16
River Ayr Walk	15 J15
River Street	12 E14
River Terrace	12 E14
River View	14 E15
Riverside Place	14 F15
Robertson Crescent	15 J14
Robertson Road	81 H4
Robsland Avenue	14 E18
Rockrose Park	17 G20
Roman Road	17 H19
Ronaldshaw Park	14 D17
Rosebank Crescent	14 E18
Rosebay Park	17 G21
Rosemount	83 H9
Gardens	
Ross Street	13 H13
Rosslyn Place	12 G12
Rowallan Court (2)	12 D14
Rowallan Crescent	83 J8
Rowan Crescent	15 H18
Rowan House (8)	12 H9
Rowanbank Road	83 K8
Rozelle Terrace	17 G22
Rush Hill	17 H21
Russell Drive	12 F13
Russell Street	12 F14
Rylands	83 H9
St Andrew's Avenue	83 H9
St Andrew's Street	14 F16
St Catherines Road	13 L13
St Cuthbert's	83 J9
Crescent	
St Cuthbert's Road	83 H9
St Georges Road	12 G12
St John Street	12 E14
(Ayr)	
St John Street	83 H7
(Prestwick)	
St Leonards Court	14 F18
St Leonard's Road	14 E18
St Leonard's Road	17 F19
St Leonards Wynd	14 E18
St Nicholas Road	82 G8
St Ninians Park	83 H8
Place	
St Ninians Road	82 G9
St Phillans Avenue	15 G17
St Quivox Road	83 H7

Name	Ref
St Vincent Crescent	17 F21
Salisbury Place	83 H7
Saltfield Lane	12 E13
Saltpans Road	12 E12
Sandfield Road	83 H7
Sandgate	14 E15
Sandyhill Road	15 K17
Sandyhill Terrace	15 K17
Sannox Place	13 J13
Sannox View	13 K13
Sanquhar Avenue	83 K8
Sanquhar Farm	13 J12
Road	
Saunterne Road	83 H6
Savoy Court	14 D16
Savoy Park	14 D16
Scaur o'Doon Road	16 B20
Sea Tower Court	14 D17
Sea Tower	14 D17
Gardens	
Seabank Road	12 D14
(Ayr)	
Seabank Road	82 G6
(Prestwick)	
Seafield Crescent	14 C17
Seafield Drive	14 C18
Seafield Road	14 D17
Seaforth Crescent	12 G11
Seaforth Road	12 G11
Seagate	81 H5
Semple Road	83 J10
Shalloch Park	12 A21
Shanter Place	16 D22
Shanter Way	16 D22
Shanter Wynd	16 D22
Shavin Brae	15 J17
Shaw Road	83 K6
Shawfarm Court	83 J6
Shawfarm Gardens	81 J5
Shawfarm Place	83 J6
Shawfarm Road	81 J5
Shawfarm Road	83 K6
Shawfield Avenue	17 F19
Sherwood Road	83 K7
Shiel Hill	17 G21
Shieling Park	14 D16
Shilliaw Drive	83 J10
Shilliaw Place	83 J10
Shillilaw Drive	83 J10
Shillilaw Place	83 J10
Shore Road	12 E12
Skye Road	83 K6
Skye Square	14 F15
Slaphouse	16 E19
Sloan Place	13 J13
Sloan Street	13 J13
Smith Street (Ayr)	14 E16
Smith Street	83 H7
(Prestwick)	
Snowdrop Square	17 G20
Somerset Gardens	12 G13
Somerset Road	12 G13
Sorrel Drive	17 H20
Souter Place	15 G18

Name	Ref
South Beach Road	12 D14
South Harbour	12 D14
Street	
South Lodge Court	14 D17
Southfield Park	14 F18
Southpark Avenue	82 G8
Southpark Road	14 D17
Southwood Road	80 F1
Spallander Crescent	17 F23
Speedwell Square	17 G20
Springbank Road	12 G11
Springfield Avenue	83 J8
Springvale Park	14 E17
Springvale Road	14 E17
Spruce House (5)	12 G10
Spruce Park	15 J18
Spur Road	12 D13
Station Bridge	14 F16
Station Drive	83 H6
Station Road (Ayr)	14 F16
Station Road	81 H2
(Monkton)	
Station Road	83 H6
(Prestwick)	
Stewart Road	12 G11
Stewartlea	14 E17
Stobhill Crescent	15 G18
Stonecrop Place	17 H19
Stonefield Park	16 B21
Strang Place	83 J10
Strathayr Place	14 E14
Strathdoon Place	16 C21
Sunningdale	17 F20
Avenue	
Sycamore Crescent	15 J17
Sym's Lane	12 F14
Taran Walk	14 F15
Tarbolton Road	81 J3, K3
Taybank Drive	17 F20
Taylor Court	12 E13
Taylor Street	12 E13
Templerigg Court	83 H6
Templerigg Street	83 H6
Templeton Crescent	83 J7
Templeton Gardens	83 J7
Teviot Square (1)	81 H5
Teviot Street	12 G12
Thistle Walk	17 H20
Thomson Street	13 H13
Thornwood Avenue	13 K13
Thornyflat Crescent	13 L13
Thornyflat Drive	13 K13
Thornyflat Place	13 L12
Thornyflat Road	13 K13
Thornyflat Street	13 K13
Tig Road	12 F12
Tilt Road	81 H4
Torbeg House (6)	12 H10
Towans Court	81 J5
Tramore Crescent	83 H7
Treebank Crescent	15 H18
Trefoil Place	17 H20
Trenchard Court (3)	12 D14
Tryfield Place	12 F13

Name	Ref
Tweed Road	81 H.
Tweed Street	12 G1
Underwood Road	83 J.
Union Arcade	14 E1.
Union Avenue	12 F1.
University Avenue	15 G1.
Upper Crofts	16 E2.
Upper Loaning	16 E2.
Victoria Crescent	13 H1
Victoria Park	14 D1
Victoria Street	12 F1
Viewfield Court	12 F1
Viewfield Road	12 F1
Virginia Gardens	12 F1
Waggon Road	12 E1
Walker Road	12 G1
Wallace Court (1)	83 J.
Wallacetown Drive	13 H1
Ward Court	12 G1
Ward Road	12 G1
Wardneuk	83 H.
Waterloo Road	12 G1.
Wattfield Road	14 E1
Weaver Street	12 E1.
Weir Avenue	83 J.
Weir Road	12 E1.
Wellington Lane	14 D1
Wellington Square	14 D1.
Wellington Street	12 G1.
Wellpark	16 E2.
Welsh Road	81 .
West Place	17 F1.
West Sanquhar	12 G1.
Avenue	
West Sanquhar	12 G1.
Place	
West Sanquhar	12 G1.
Road	
Westbourne Avenue	83 .
Westbourne	83 .
Gardens	
Westfield Road	14 D.
Weston Place	83 H.
Westwood Avenue	15 J.
Westwood Crescent	13 K.
Wexford Way (7)	12 D.
Wheatfield Road	14 D.
Wheatpark Place	13 L.
Wheatpark Road	13 K.
Whin Hill Road	17 G.
Whinfield Avenue	83 H.
Whinfield Gardens	83 H.
Whinfield Place	83 H.
Whinfield Road	82 G.
White Street	12 F.
Whiteford View	15 J.
Whitehall Avenue	83 .
Whiteside Cottages	81 .
Whiteside Drive	81 .
Whiteside Gardens	81 .
Whiteside Park	81 .
Whiteside Place	81 .
Whiteside Road	83 .
Whiteside Terrace	83 .

hitfield Drive	13 J12	Ash Walk	43 M3
hitletts Court	13 K13	Ashgrove	42 E4
hitletts Road	12 G14	Auchenharvie Place	42 H3
hittle Road	13 H12	Avon Court	43 J5
illow Park	17 H19	Ayr Road	45 E8
ills Gardens	13 H13	Ayr Road	48 E10
ills Road	13 H13	Balgray Way	43 J3
ilson Street	12 G13	Ballot Road	45 E6
indward Park	17 F22	Bank Court	42 G5
inston Avenue	83 J8	Bank Place	42 G5
ood Park (Ayr)	17 G19	Bank Street	42 G5
ood Park	83 H8	Bank Street	45 E7, F7
(Prestwick)		Bankhead Avenue	47 Q6
oodend Road	16 E22	Barbeth Place	43 J4
oodfield Avenue	12 F10	Barclay Gardens	43 M3
oodfield Crescent	12 F11	Barony Court	42 H5
oodfield Lane	12 G10	Barr Crescent	42 E5
oodfield Road	12 F11	Barra Crescent	46 L7
oodlands	17 G19	Barra Lane	46 L7
Crescent		Barra Place	46 L7
oodlands Street	82 G7	Barra Wynd	46 L7
oodlea Place	17 G21	Bartonholm	41 B3
ightfield Place	16 D21	Gardens	
yburn Place	12 F12	Beaton Terrace	42 E4
omanry Place	12 D14	Beech Avenue	45 F7
rk Place	12 E13	Beech Drive	44 B8
rk Street	12 E13	Belfast Quay	44 C7
rk Street Lane	12 E13	Bell Crescent	42 F4
ung Street	12 G10	Benbain Place	43 K3
unger Drive	81 H5	Bencleuch Place	46 K6
		Bensley Avenue	42 H4
dex to Irvine,		Bensley Rise	42 H4
eghorn & Springside		Benthill Terrace	44 C8
		Beresford Grove	42 G4
erfeldy Terrace	43 J3	Berry Drive	45 G6
erlour Place	42 H3	Berryhill Avenue	43 K3
erlour Road	42 H3	Bilby Terrace	42 E4
ademy Court	44 D6	Bimson Place	44 C8
ademy Gardens	41 D5	Bimson Row	44 C8
ademy Road	44 D6	Birks Hill	43 J5
ams Walk	45 G7	Birkscairn Place	46 L7
on Court	44 D7	Birkscairn Way	46 L7
sa Road	44 C10, D10	Blairdenon Way	46 K7
ler Green	43 J5	Blaven Head	43 J5
xander Place	41 D5	Bluebell View	43 M3
ord Place	42 G4	Bodesbeck Court	46 J6
an Square	45 G6	Bonnyton Foot	43 J4
derson Drive	42 F4	Bonnyton Place	43 J4
nandale Way	43 J4	Bonnyton Row	43 K4
nfield Gardens	44 D8	Bowhouse Head	43 J4
nick Court	45 E7	Bowhouse Rise	43 K4
nick Drive	46 K8	Bowmore Court	43 J3
nick Road	46 K8	Boyle Street	44 C7
Dreghorn)		Bradbury Glebe	45 E7
nick Road	45 F7, G8	Braefoot	42 H4
rvine)		Braehead	42 H4
nick View	45 G7	Braeside	42 H4
hers Avenue	42 G3	Brewster Place	46 H10
hers Court	42 G3	Brice Knox Court	43 J3
lbeg Court	42 H3	Bridgegate	45 E7
lmore Court	43 J3	Broomlands Busway	45 G7
wright Way	45 H6	Broomlands Busway	46 J7
an Place	41 D4	Broomlands Court	46 J7
anview Court	44 D6	Broomlands Drive	45 F7

Broomlands Gate	46 J7	Corsehill Mount	46 J8, K9
Broomlands Place	45 F7	Road	
Broomlands Road	46 K8	Corsehill Park	47 M9
Broughton Green	43 K3	Corsehill Terrace	47 N7
Brown Walk	42 F4	Corserine Bank	46 H6
Bruce Terrace	42 F4	Cotton Row	45 E7
Burnbrae Crescent	43 L4	Craig View	47 P7
Burnbrae Drive	43 L4	Craigmark Place	42 H4
Burns Crescent	43 J4	Craignaw Place	46 K7
Burns Street	44 D6	Cramalt Court	46 J6
Burnside Place	41 D4	Cramond Place	46 H7
Busbiehead (2)	43 K4	Cramond Way	46 H7
Bute Court	46 L8	Craven Grove	42 H4
Cairngorm Court	43 K4	Crocus Grove	41 E5
Cairnmount Road	42 H2	Crocus Grove	45 E6
Cairnsgarroch Way	46 K7	Croft Terrace	47 P7
Cairnsmore Way	46 K7	Crofthead	46 J6
Caldon Road	42 E5	Crofthead Court	46 J6
Campbell Place	46 K9	Crompton Way	42 G5
Campsie Avenue	46 K6	Crompton Way	45 G6
Campsie Walk	46 K6	Cuillin Place	43 J5
Campsie Way	46 J7	Cumbrae Court	46 L8
Capel Place	46 K7	Cunninghame Road	44 D9
Capringstone Foot	43 K4	Cypress Gardens	42 G4
Cardon Place	46 K7	Dale Crescent	42 F5
Cardow Crescent	43 J3	Dalgain Court	43 J4
Carmel Drive	47 Q8	Dalmailing Avenue	46 K8
Carmichael Place	41 D4	Dalmore Place	42 H3
Carnoustie Place	45 G10	Dalmore Way	42 H3
Carrick Drive	41 D4	Dalrymple Drive	45 F6
Carron Place	42 E3	Dalrymple Place	45 F6
Carson Drive	45 E9	Dalwhinnie Court	42 H3
Carters Place	45 E7	Dalyrymple Court	45 G6
Carters Rigg	44 D8	Darnshaw Close	43 L4
Castle Keep	42 H5	Dick Crescent	42 F4
Gardens		Dick Terrace	42 F4
Castle Place	44 D6	Dickson Drive	41 D4
Castle Street	44 D6	Dickson Drive	42 E4
Castlepark Circle	42 E3	Donaldson Drive	42 F5
Castlepark Crescent	41 D3	Doon Court	45 E7
Castlepark Road	41 D3	Doura Drive	42 H4
Cedar Road	42 F5	Doura Place	42 E4
Centenary Court	46 H10	Dreghorn Road	47 M10
Centenary Road	45 H9	Drumelzier Court	43 J5
Centenary Road	46 H10	Drummond	45 G10
Century Court	46 H10	Crescent	
Chalmers Place	49 H11	Drummond	46 H10
Chapel Lane	45 E7	Crescent	
Chapelgill Place	43 J5	Drumuir Foot	43 K4
Cherry Gardens	42 G4	Dublin Quay	44 C7
Chestnut Gardens	42 G4	Duncan Drive	45 F7
Cheviot Court	46 J6	Dundonald Road	46 L8
Cheviot Head	46 H6	Dunlop Crescent	46 K8
Cheviot Way	46 J6	Dunlop Drive	48 G13
Church Street	44 D7	Dunlop Place	49 H13
Clark Drive	42 G5	Duntonknoll	42 E5
Clark Drive	45 F7	Dunvegan Place	42 F3
Clayton Avenue	42 E5	Earncraig Green	46 J6
Coach Brae View	47 N7	Earls Bridge	42 G2
Cochrane Street	44 D7	Gardens	
Cockburn Place	49 H11	Earls Bridge Place	42 G2
Coleburn Court	42 H3	Earlswood Avenue	42 G4
Coll Gardens	46 K9	Earlswood View	42 G3
Corse Avenue	47 Q8	Earlswood Way	42 G3

Index to Irvine, Dreghorn, Springside & Kilwinning

Name	Ref
Earlswood Wynd	42 G3
East Bowhouse Head	43 K4
East Bowhouse Way	43 K4
East Broomlands	46 K7
East Road	45 E6, E7
Eastwood Avenue	42 F5
Eglinton Gardens	45 E6
Eglinton Street	45 E6
Elmbank Terrace	42 F5
Eriskay Court	46 L9
Esplanade	44 B8
Etive Place	42 F4
Fairlie Drive	43 K3
Fairways, The	41 C2
Fencedyke Close	42 H5
Fencedyke Way	43 J5
Fencedyke Way	46 J6
Finnie Terrace	47 P7
Fintry Place	46 K7
Fintry Terrace	46 K6
Fintry Walk	46 K7
First Avenue	45 E9
Fleming Terrace	41 D4
Ford Avenue	47 M8
Fortacre Place	43 K4
Frew Terrace	42 E4
Friar's Croft	44 D7
Fullarton Street	44 D7
Gailes Road	48 E12, E13
Galt Avenue	45 F6
Gardens, The	43 L3
Garelet Place	46 K7
Garnock Court	45 E7
Garrier Court	47 P7
Garrier Road	47 P7
Gateside	42 H3
George Court	45 E6
George Terrace	45 E6
Gigha Crescent	46 K7
Gigha Lane	46 K7
Gigha Place	46 K7
Gigha Terrace	46 K7
Gigha Wynd	46 K7
Gilbertfield Place	45 F7
Girdle Gate	42 H4
Glasgow Vennel	45 E7
Glebe Avenue	46 L9
Glebe, The	46 L8, 46 L9
Glenbervie Wynd	45 F9
Gleneagles Place	45 F10
Glenleith Place	46 L7
Glenlyon Grove	42 H4
Goldcraig Court	43 J4
Golf Place	41 D4
Golffields Road	45 F8
Gottries Place	44 C8
Gottries Road	44 C8
Grampian Court	43 K5
Grange, The	43 L3
Gray Crescent	45 E9
Green Avenue	42 E5
Greenbank Court	45 E8
Greenbank Road	45 E8
Greenfield Drive	45 F7
Greenhill Court	43 K3
Greenside	43 J5
Greenside Avenue	47 P8
Greenside Terrace	47 Q7
Greenside Way	43 J5
Greenwood Gate	46 J8
Greenwood Road	46 L8
Gullane Court	45 F9
Gulliland Place	45 F8
Haddington Gardens	43 K3
Harbour Road	44 C8
Harbour Street	44 C8
Harris Court	46 L9
Harris Terrace	46 L9
Heatherhouse Road	44 D9
Heatherstane Bank	46 K7
Heatherstane Walk (1)	46 L7
Heatherstane Way	46 L7
Hepburn Way	43 L2
Herbertson Crescent	42 F5
High Street	45 E7
Highet Gardens	41 D5
Highfield Place	42 H3
Hill Street	45 E7
Hillshaw Foot	46 L7
Hillshaw Green	46 L7
Holms Avenue	47 M8
Holms Farm Cottages	47 M10
Hopetoun Bank	46 L7
Howat Crescent	45 G6
Hunter Drive	41 D3
Inverleven Place	42 H2
Iona Court	46 L9
Iona Place	46 L9
Irvine Mains Crescent	42 E5
Irvine Road	41 C1
Islay Court	46 L9
James Crescent	41 D5
Jermond Drive	42 F4
John Galt Crescent	42 F5
John Galt Drive	42 F5
John Galt Wynd	42 F5
Jura Court	46 L9
Kames Court	43 K3
Katrine Place	42 F3
Kennedy Park	46 K9
Kerr Drive	45 F7
Kerr Place	45 F7
Kersland Foot	42 H4
Kidsneuk	41 C3
Kidsneuk Gardens	41 C3
Killoch Place	42 H5
Killoch Way	42 H5
Kilmarnock Road	47 Q7
Kiln Court	45 E7
Kiln Walk	45 E7
Kilpatrick Court	46 J6
Kilpatrick Place	46 J7
Kilsyth Crescent	46 J6
Kilsyth Walk	46 J6
Kilwinning Road	41 C2, D5
Kirk Vennel	45 E7
Kirkgate	45 E7
Kirkhill	43 L3
Kirkland Terrace	47 P7
Kirkstyle Court	43 K3
Knockentiber Road	47 Q7
Kyle Avenue	47 P7
Kyle Road	44 D9, D10
Ladyacre Court	42 G3
Ladyacre Grove	42 G3
Ladyacre View	42 G3
Ladyacre Way	42 G3
Ladyburn Court	42 H3
Ladyha Court	43 K4
Lamberton Gardens	43 L4
Lammermuir Court	46 J6
Lamont Drive	45 E9
Lamont Place	45 E9
Lanfine Row	43 J3
Lanfine Terrace	42 H3
Lanfine Way	43 J3
Langmuir Avenue	43 L4
Langmuir Court	43 L4
Lawers Place	43 J5
Lawthorn Road	43 K3
Leven Place	42 F3
Lewis Court	46 J7
Lewis Crescent	46 H7
Lewis Rise	46 J7
Lewis Terrace	46 J7
Lewis Wynd	46 J7
Lime Way	43 M3
Linkwood Court	43 J3
Linkwood Place	43 J3
Linthouse Vennel	44 C8
Lismore Drive	46 K9
Lismore Way	46 L9
Littlestane Court	43 J3
Littlestane Rise	43 J3
Littlestane Road	42 H3
Littlestane Road	43 J3
Littlestane Row	43 J3
Livingstone Terrace	42 E4
Loach Avenue	45 F8
Lochcraig Court	46 J6
Lochlibo Court	43 J3
Lochlibo Road	42 H4
Lochlibo Road	43 J1
Lochwood Place	42 H3
Lomond Place	42 F3
Lomond Way	43 J5
Long Drive	42 H4
Long Drive	46 H7
Long Drive	49 J12
Longrow Gardens	42 H2
Loudoun Rigg	45 E8
Low Green Road	44 D6
Lower Vennel (1)	46 J6
Lowther Bank	46 L6
Lugar Avenue	43 J3
Lugton Court	45
Lyle Gardens	45
MacAdam Place	46
MacAllen Place	42
MacKinnon Terrace	42
MacKintosh Place	46
MacRedie Place	43
MacRobert Avenue	46
McClure Gardens	45
McDonald Drive	42
McGibney Drive	45
McKinlay Crescent	44
McLean Drive	47
McMillan Place	49 H
Macara Drive	45
Malcolm Gardens	45
Maid Morville Avenue	46
Main Road	47
Main Street	46
Mansfield Way	43
Manson Road	42
Manuel Court	46
Manuel Terrace	46
Maple Terrace	42
Marble Avenue	47
Maree Place	42
Marine Drive	44
Marine Drive	48
Marress Road	44
Martin Avenue	42
Maxwell Green	43
Maxwood Place	43
Meadow Avenue	42
Meadowhead Avenue	48 G
Meadowhead Road	49 H
Meadows, The	41
Meikle Place	43
Merrick Place	46
Merryvale Road	45
Metcalfe Place	49 H
Mid Rig	43
Middleton Park	43
Middleton Road	43
Milbank Row	47
Milgarholm Avenue	45
Mill Crescent	45
Mill Road	45
Millburn Terrace	43
Milldown Place	46
Millfore Court	46
Milton Court	47
Milton Crescent	46
Milton Road	46
Monach Gardens	46
Montgomery Lane	44
Montgomery Place	44
Montgomery Street	44
Montgomeryfield	46
Moorfoot Place	46
Moorfoot Way	46
Morar Place	42

oss Drive	48 G12	Ranken Drive	45 F6
ossgiel Drive	45 F6	Rannoch Place	41 D2
ount View	46 L8	Rannoch Place	42 E3
uir Drive	45 F6	Ravenscroft	41 D4
uirfield Court	45 G10	Redburn Gate	41 C2
uirhall Place	46 L8	Redburn Place	41 D3
ull Court	46 J7	Regalia View	42 G3
ull Crescent	46 J7	Renton Park	43 L2
ull Place	46 J7	Rig Foot	43 K4
ull Terrace	46 J7	Riverside Avenue	46 J10
urchland Way	44 D6	Riverside Road	47 M8
urdoch Place	49 H11	Riverside Way	45 G9
eil Avenue	42 F4	Riverway	44 D8
evis Way	43 J5	Ronaldsay Court	46 K9
ew Street	44 D7	Rosebank Gardens	42 H2
ewfield Place	43 K4	Roseholm Avenue	45 G7
ewhouse Way	43 J4	Rowan Terrace	42 F5
ewtonhead (1)	43 K4	Rowantree Gardens	43 J4
erman Crescent	41 D4	Rubie Crescent	45 E9
orth Vennel	46 J6	St Andrew's Way	45 F9
ursery Gardens	47 Q7	St Bride's Place	42 E4
aklands Avenue	42 E5	St Inan Avenue	45 G6
chil Court	43 J4	St Kilda Bank	46 J7
d Caley Road	42 E4, E5	St Kilda Court	46 J7
miston Place	43 L2	St Kilda Place	46 J7
erton Place	43 K4	Sanderson	44 D8
ertoun Court	47 Q7	Avenue	
ertoun Road	47 P6	Sandy Road	41 B2, C4
ddock, The	43 L3	Sandy Road	41 C3
rk Place	41 D4	Place	
rkside	46 K6	School Lane	45 E8
rterre	45 E7	Scott Road	45 E8
terson Avenue	42 F4, F5	Seagate	44 D6
terson	42 F4	Seaton Terrace	41 D4
rescent		Seaton Terrace	42 E4
vilion Gardens	42 G3	Second Avenue	44 E9
den Place	45 E7	Shalloch Place	46 K7
nbreck Court	43 K3	Sharpe Avenue	47 M9
nnant Court	42 G3	Shawholm Gardens	45 E6
nnant Place	42 G2	Shewalton Road	45 F10
nnant Way	42 G3	Shewalton Road	49 J11
nnyvenie Way	43 J4	Shiel Place	42 E3
ntland Place	46 J6	Shielhope Court	43 J5
rceton Mains	43 M3	Sidlaw Foot	46 L7
rceton Row	47 M6	Sillars Meadow	45 G7
ter Street	44 C8	Skye Court	46 K9
rsland Place	43 J4	Slate Mill Gardens	45 G7
dda Avenue	46 J7	Sloan Avenue	45 F7
dda Court	46 K7	Smiddy Close	45 E6
dda Crescent	46 J7	Smith Avenue	42 F5
dda Terrace	46 K7	Smithstone Court	42 H4
dda Wynd	46 J7	Smithstone Way	42 H3
tland Avenue	44 D9	Somerville Park	43 K2
tland Place	44 D9	Somerville Way	43 K2
tland Road	44 C9	Sophia Crescent	41 D3
dle Ford	45 E7	Sourlie Terrace	42 H4
dies Close	45 E7	Southook Row	43 J4
arry Road	45 E6	South Newmoor	45 G8
een Road	42 E4	Avenue	
een's Court	45 F7	South Newmoor	46 H8
cecourse Place	41 C4	Avenue	
nstane Place	43 L4	South Vennel (2)	46 J6
ken Crescent	45 F6	Speyburn Place	42 H3
ken Drive	42 F5	Springbank Gardens	43 J2

Springfield Gardens	43 J2	West Court	44 D7
Springhill Terrace	47 P7	West Road	44 D6
Springside Terrace	47 N7	Whitehope Green	46 J6
Staffa Court	46 K9	Whitewisp Court	43 J5
Stanecastle Drive	42 G4	Whittle Place	46 H7
Stanecastle Gate	42 H4	Whyte Avenue	45 F8
Stanecastle Road	42 H5	William Burns Place	46 L8
Station Brae	46 L8	Williamfield Park	41 D5
Station Brae	46 L8	Williamsfield Grove	41 D5
Gardens		Willow Gardens	42 G4
Station Drive	47 P6	Wilson Avenue	42 E5
Station Road	47 P7	Windelstraw Court	46 J6
Steadman Place	46 J9	Winton Place	42 E5
Steps Road	42 E4	Wood Grove	46 L8
Stewart Drive	42 F5	Woodhill Crescent	43 K3
Strathmore Park	43 K3	Woodlands Avenue	45 F6
Stroma Court	46 L9	Wyvis Place	43 J5
Stronsay Court	46 J7		
Stronsay Way	46 J7	**Index to Kilwinning**	
Swinton Place	43 K2		
Sycamore Wynd	43 M3	Abbey View	62 B3
Symington Place	46 H10	Abbeygate	63 E4
Tarryholme Drive	45 E7	Abbeygreen	63 E4
Tay Place	42 E3	Abbot's Avenue	63 E5
Telford Place	46 H8	Abbot's Place	63 E4
Third Avenue	44 D9	Abbot's Walk	63 E4
Thornhouse Avenue	45 F6	Ainsdale Court	62 A4
Thornhouse Court	45 F6	Alexandra Gardens	62 D4
Thornwood Drive	45 E7	Alexandra Terrace	62 D4
Tiree Court	46 K9	Almswall Road	63 E4
Titchfield Way	43 J4	Annanhill Place	62 B4
Tollerton Drive	42 F5	Ardmillan	62 B5
Tollhouse Way	43 J4	Ashenyards Park	62 A5
Towerlands Farm	42 H5	Ashgrove Road	62 C3
Road		Atholl Gardens	63 E3
Towerlands Farm	46 J6	Auchenkist Place	62 D2
Road		Baberton Way	62 B4
Towerlands Farm	46 K7	Baird Avenue	63 E3
Road		Bankhead Road	63 F4
Towerlands Gate	46 K7	Bannoch Cottages	63 G2
Towerlands Road	46 J6, L7	Bannoch Gardens	63 G3
Townfoot	46 K9	Bannoch Place	63 G4
Townfoot Lane	46 K8	Bannoch Road	63 G2, G4
Townhead	45 F7	Bannoch Road	63 G5
Turnberry Wynd	45 F9	Bargeny	62 B5
Victoria Crescent	44 D8	Bartonholm	63 F6
Vineburgh Avenue	42 E5	Terrace	
Vineburgh Court	41 D5	Beechwood	62 D2
Vines, The	42 E5	Belleisle Close	62 C3
Wallace Road	42 E5	Bevan Gardens	63 E3
Wardlaw Gardens	43 K2	Birkdale Close	62 C3
Wardneuk Court	43 J3	Birklands Wynd	62 B3
Warrix Avenue	45 F7	Blacklands Avenue	63 E5
Warwickhill	43 K4	Blacklands Crescent	63 E6
Watercut Road	41 B1	Blair Road	63 F3
Waterside	44 D6	Blairafton Wynd	62 C2
Watson Terrace	45 F7	Braid Court	62 B4
Weavers Wynd	45 E6	Braidwood Road	63 E3
West Bowhouse	43 J4	Bridgend Lane	63 F4
Gardens		Bridgend	63 F4
West Bowhouse	43 J4	Brodick Avenue	62 C3
Head		Brodick Close	62 C2
West Bowhouse	43 J4	Broomfield Street	63 E2
Way		Broomhill Court	62 C2

Index to Kilwinning

Bruntsfield Avenue	62 B4	Foundry Court	62 C3
Burns Place	63 F4	Foundry Wynd	62 C3
Busbie Place	63 F3	Friars Lawn	62 D4
Byrehill Avenue (Blacklands)	63 E5	Gagarin Terrace	63 E5
		Ganton Court	62 B4
Byrehill Avenue (West Byrehill)	62 B5	Garden Lane	63 E4
		Garden Square	63 E4
Byrehill Drive	62 A5	Garnock View	63 E3
Byrehill Place	62 B5	Garrallan	62 C5
Byrehill Road	62 C6	Glebe Street	63 E3
Byres Loch	62 D4	Glenapp Court	62 C5
Byres Road	62 D4	Glenapp Place	62 C5
Calderwood	63 E2	Glenbervie Drive	62 B4
Cambusdoon Place	62 D4	Glenburn Close	62 C1
Carnoustie Court	62 B4	Gleneagles Avenue	62 C3
Cartle Close	62 C1	Graystones	63 E2
Cartleburn Gardens	62 D2	Greenfoot	63 E4
Cassiland Place	62 B3	Groatholm Way	62 D2
Castlehill Farm	62 A4	Gullane Place	62 B4
Cathkin Place	62 B3	Hamilton Court	63 E3
Chalybeate Court	62 D4	Hamilton Street	63 E3
Church Street	63 E4	Hawthorn Place	63 E5
Churchill Avenue	63 F3	Hawthorn Court	63 E5
Claremont Crescent	62 D3	Hazeldene Park	63 F3
Clonbeith Court	62 D2	Hazel Grove	63 G3
Cloncaird	62 C5	Helen's Terrace	63 E5
Coodham Place	62 D4	Heronswood	63 E2
Corsehill	63 F4	Highfield Street	63 F3
Cranberry Court	62 C4	Hillcrest Place	63 F4
Cranberry Head	62 C4	Hillpark Rise	62 B4
Cranberry Moss Road	62 C6	Howden Avenue	63 E3
		Howgate	62 D4
Cranberry Moss Road	62 D4	Hoylake Square	62 C3
		Hunter Place	63 G4
Cranberry Place	62 C4	Innerwood Road	63 E2
Cranberry Road	62 B5	Irvine Road	63 F5
Crannog Way	62 C3	James Clement's Close	62 C3
Culzean Place	62 C5		
Dalgarven Wynd	62 C2	Keir Hardie Crescent	63 G4
Daljarrock	62 B5		
Dalmahoy Way	62 B4	Kelburne	62 C5
Dalry Road	62 D2	Kelvin Avenue	63 F6
Darmule Drive	62 C2	Kilkerran	62 C4
David Gage Street	63 E2	Killermont Place	62 B4
Davids Crescent	62 D5	Kilrig Avenue	63 E3
Deanfield Court	63 E4	Kilwinning Gates	63 G6
Dirrans Terrace	63 F5	King Street	63 E3
Dornoch Court	62 B4	Kinnis Vennel	62 C3
Dovecot Lane	63 F4	Kirkhill	62 C5
Druid Drive	63 E3	Knights Bridge House	63 H6
Dubbs Road	62 A6		
Duddingston Avenue	62 B3	Kyleswell Street	63 E4
Dunure Court	62 D4	Ladyacre	63 E3
Dykehead Cottages	63 G6	Ladyford Avenue	63 E4
Eden Court	62 B4	Lainshaw	62 C5
Edzell Row	62 B4	Lauchlan Way	63 E4
Eglinton Place	63 E4	Lissens Walk	62 C2
Enterkine	62 B5	Lochwood Close	62 C2
Evelyn Terrace	62 D5	Longford Avenue	63 E6
Fairhaven Square	62 B3	Loudoun Crescent	62 B3
Fergushill Road	63 F4	Love Street	63 G4
Fir Tree Place	63 G3	McGavin Avenue	63 G4
Five Roads	63 G4	McGavin Way	62 D3
Forge Vennel	62 C3	McLuckie Drive	62 C4

McLuckie Park	62 C3	St Winning's Lane	63 E
Machrie Place	62 C4	St Winning's Well	62 D
Main Street	63 E4	St Joan's Crescent	63 E
Main Street	63 F4	Segton Avenue	62 C
Manse Court	63 E4	Seymour Avenue	63 F
Matthew Place	63 E2	Shavian Terrace	63 E
Meadows, The	62 D3	Simpson Place	63 F
Meadow Park Road	62 C2, C3	Skelmorlie Place	62 D
		Smiddy Court	63 E
Meadow View	62 C2	Smith Crescent	63 F
Meadow Way	62 C2	Station Plaza	62 D
Millside Gardens	63 F4	Stevenston Road	62 E
Moncur Court	62 C2	Stobbs Crescent	63 E
Moncur Road	63 G4	Stobbs Terrace	63 E
Monkreddan Crescent	62 C2	Sundrum Place	62 D
		Sunningdale Square	62 C
Montgomerie Terrace	63 G4	Sutton Court	62 E
Montgreenan View	63 F4	Tammy Dale's Road	63 F
Morville Crescent	63 E2		
Mountcastle Wynd	62 C1	Thornhill Court	62 E
Muirfield Place	62 C3	Townhead	62 D
Muirside Court	62 C5	Treesbank	62 C
Muirside Place	62 C5	Turnberry Court	62 E
Muirside Road	62 C5	Underwood	62 E
Muirside Steadings	62 A5	Vaults Lane	63 F
Nairn Court	62 B4	Viaduct Circle	63 F
Nethermains Road	63 E5	Wallwood	62 E
Newark	62 C5	Waterside Road	63 F
Ninian's Terrace	63 F5	Weirston Road	63 E
Northacre	63 E2	Wentworth Square	62 E
Northacre Grove	63 E2	West Doura Court	62 E
Nursery Drive	62 C2	West Doura Way	62 C
Nursery Wynd	62 C2	Whitehirst Park Road	62 E
Old Glasgow Road	63 G3		
Old Woodwynd Road	62 D3	Winstanley Wynd	62 E
		Winton Avenue	62 E
Orchard Grove	63 E3	Wood Crescent	63
Orchard Place	63 E3	Wood Street	63
Oxenward Road	63 E4	Woodburn Avenue	63
Park Avenue	63 E4	Woodfarm Close	62
Park Lane	62 D2	Woodgreen Wynd	62
Parkhead Avenue	63 F4	Woodmill	63
Pathfoot	63 F4	Woodside Road	62
Pathfoot View	63 F4	Woodside Road	62
Papingo Close	62 C1	Woodwynd	63
Pennyburn Road	62 B5		
Pennyburn Road	62 D4		
Pinmore	62 C5		
Pollock Crescent	63 E5		
Prestonfield Avenue	62 B3		
Priory Wynd	62 C1		
Queen Street	63 G4		
Queens Place	63 G4		
Redstone Avenue	63 F3		
Redstone Wynd	63 G3		
River Walk	63 E2		
Robert W Service Court	63 E5		
Rosemount	62 C5		
Rowallan	62 C5		
St Michael's Wynd	62 C4		
St Winning's Road	62 D4		
St Winning's Road	63 E4